IT Infrastructure Library

STACK HOUSE
SQUIRES CLOSE
SHEFFORD
BEDFORDSHIRE SG17 5JB

A Guide to Business Continuity Management

LONDON: THE STATIONERY OFFICE

Acknowledgements   The assistance of Simon Marvell under contract to CCTA from Insight Consulting is gratefully acknowledged.

© **Crown Copyright 1995**   First published by HMSO 1995
Fourth impression published by The Stationery Office 1999

Published by permission of the Central Computer and Telecommunications Agency under licence from the Controller of HMSO

Applications for reproduction should be made to
The Copyright Unit
Her Majesty's Stationery Office
St Clements House, 2-16 Colegate
Norwich NR3 1BQ

ISBN 0 11 330675 X

For further information regarding CCTA products please contact:

CCTA Library
Rosebery Court
St Andrews Business Park
Norwich
NR7 0HS
01603 704930

Contents

Chapter		page
1	**Introduction**	7
	1.1 Purpose of this volume	
	1.2 Who should read this volume	
	1.3 Structure of the volume	
2	**Overview of the BCM lifecycle**	11
3	**Stage 1 of the lifecycle – Initiation**	15
	3.1 Set policy	
	3.2 Specify terms of reference and scope	
	3.3 Allocate resources	
	3.4 Define project organisation and control structure	
	3.5 Agree project and quality plans	
4	**Stage 2 of the lifecycle – Requirements and strategy**	21
	4.1 Business impact analysis	
	4.2 Risk assessment	
	4.3 Business continuity strategy	
5	**Stage 3 of the lifecycle – Implementation**	49
	5.1 Establish organisation and develop implementation plans	
	5.2 Implement stand-by arrangements	
	5.3 Implement risk reduction measures	
	5.4 Develop business recovery plans(s)	
	5.5 Develop procedures	
	5.6 Carry out initial tests	
6	**Stage 4 of the lifecycle – Operational management**	83
	6.1 Testing	
	6.2 Education and awareness	
	6.3 Training	
	6.4 Review and change control	
	6.5 Assurance	
	6.6 Key milestones in business continuity management	

7	**Skills and techniques**	97
	7.1 Stage 1 – Initiation	
	7.2 Stage 2 – Requirements and strategy	
	7.3 Stage 3 – Implementation	
	7.4 Stage 4 – Operational management	
8	**Methods and tools**	101
	8.1 Stage 1 – Initiation	
	8.2 Stage 2 – Requirements and strategy	
	8.3 Stage 3 – Implementation	
	8.4 Stage 4 – Operational management	
9	**Common applications of BCM**	109
	9.1 Centralised environment	
	9.2 Distributed environment	
	9.3 Outsourced functions or processes including dependency on external services	
	Bibliography	129
	Glossary	133
Annexes		
A	List of activities by process	139
B	Sample product descriptions and quality criteria	143
C	ABC Organisation – business recovery plan template for the XYZ Processes	149
D	Example application of Annual Loss Expectancy (ALE)	175
	Index	177

Contents

List of figures

Figure 1	Business continuity management process model	14
Figure 2	Graphical representation of business impacts	29
Figure 3	Sample form for recording minimum requirements	31
Figure 4	Sample form for recording minimum requirements for computer systems and networks	32
Figure 5	Consolidated recovery requirements for people, assets and services	33
Figure 6	Typical risks	35
Figure 7	Typical recovery options	41
Figure 8	Typical risk reduction measures	47
Figure 9	Typical command control and communications structure	50
Figure 10	Typical responsibilities for members of the central co-ordination team	52
Figure 11	Typical structure and content of business recovery plans	56
Figure 12	Typical 'logical' set of integrated business recovery plans	58
Figure 13	Sample team structure for a computer systems and networks business recovery plan	65
Figure 14	Typical contents of business recovery plans for key support services and critical business processes	73
Figure 15	Typical review changes	89
Figure 16	Typical maintenance changes	91
Figure 17	Variation on benefit with risk	176

A Guide to Business Continuity Management

1 Introduction

1.1 Purpose of this volume

It is vitally important to the success of any organisation that it can continue to carry on its business without interruption. In the public sector the drivers for doing this include providing services to the levels laid down in citizens' charters. In the private sector the growth of market share and increasing profitability are critical success factors. In both sectors, therefore, it is important that organisations plan in advance to ensure they can continue to function in the event of fire, flood or other disaster. That discipline is called business continuity management (BCM).

Traditionally, when information technology (IT) is provided centrally, ie in a predominately mainframe environment, responsibility for contingency planning rests with the IT service provider. However, with most business activities now being supported by distributed processing using PCs, local area networks and minicomputer systems, ie IT delivered to the desktop, the emphasis for planning for continuity has moved into the business areas.

Planning for continuity will enable the recovery of critical business processes. Plans will cover the people who run the business processes and the accommodation, IT, telecommunications, infrastructure services and manual records that support them.

This volume describes the processes involved in BCM and outlines the techniques, methods and tools that can be applied and the skills that are required.

The volume is structured as an in-depth implementation guide which is applicable generally to all organisations and business processes. Specific guidance is also provided for common applications of BCM, such as where:

- business processes are centralised or there is a high dependency on centralised IT services
- business processes are distributed across more than one geographic location or there is a high dependency on distributed IT services and networks

IT Infrastructure Library
A Guide to Business Continuity Management

- there is a high dependency on telecommunications or other third party provided services outside the direct control of the organisation

- business functions or processes have been, or are being, outsourced.

The guidance draws on practical experience of BCM in both the public and private sectors.

1.2 Who should read this volume

The volume is intended for managers who are responsible for the delivery of business processes and business functions, including:

- managers of key business processes (such as marketing, sales and customer services) who have responsibility for the continuity and performance of individual processes

- managers of key support functions such as IT, office services and telecommunications who have responsibility for the continuity and performance of underpinning functions

- those responsible for specifying and managing services from external providers.

In particular, this volume provides guidance to managers:

- responsible for *establishing and managing BCM projects* on how accurately to specify activities and produce detailed project plans

- *undertaking BCM projects* and *producing BCM deliverables* on
    - how to address BCM processes and activities
    - issues to consider and pitfalls to avoid
    - the recommended structure and content of BCM deliverables

- *reviewing BCM deliverables* on issues to consider and question, and quality criteria for BCM deliverables

- *performing BCM operational management processes* on how to establish and operate these processes.

This guidance may also be of interest to people in the management services and IS/IT services industry.

Chapter 1
Introduction

1.3 Structure of the volume

The remainder of the volume is structured into a further eight chapters describing how to implement BCM:

- Chapter 2 provides an overview of BCM and introduces the four stages of the BCM lifecycle
- Chapters 3 to 6 describe how to address the four stages of the lifecycle – initiation; requirements and strategy; implementation; and operational management
- Chapter 7 outlines the skills and techniques required to implement BCM effectively
- Chapter 8 describes methods and tools that can assist with implementation of BCM
- Chapter 9 gives specific advice on how to apply BCM to common business situations, such as where business processes are being outsourced.

1.4 Other related guidance

This *Guide to Business Continuity Management* is complemented by an *Introduction to Business Continuity Management* which:

- describes the need for BCM and introduces the processes involved
- describes typical management structures for BCM
- explains how to establish a BCM initiative and how to generate awareness and commitment.

The *Guide* and the *Introduction* are volumes from the CCTA IT Infrastructure Library.

Business continuity management issues are also highlighted in a CCTA briefing pamphlet for senior management: *Safeguarding the Business – The Role of Business Continuity Management*.

IT Infrastructure Library
A Guide to Business Continuity Management

2 Overview of the BCM lifecycle

The modern business environment is characterised by *risk*. Organisations define objectives, develop strategies and set targets and budgets, but even the best laid plans can be shattered by unforeseen events. Unfortunately, the chances of an organisation suffering a major disruption to its business are real – the incidence of terrorism, disasters, fraud and commercial espionage have all increased in recent years.

Where a disruption affects critical business processes the consequences can be severe and include substantial financial loss, embarrassment and loss of credibility or goodwill for the organisation concerned. The consequential damage can extend much wider; impacting on staff welfare, customers, suppliers, tax payers, shareholders and the general public.

BCM is concerned with managing risks to ensure that at all times an organisation can continue operating to, at least, a predetermined minimum level.

The risks to be addressed by BCM are those that could result in a sudden and serious disruption to the business, for example:

- damage or denial of access to premises, perhaps as a result of terrorism, fire, flood or other physical disasters
- loss of critical underpinning services such as telecommunications and power
- failure or non-performance of critical suppliers, distributors or other third parties, particularly where key business functions have been outsourced
- human error, technical or environmental breakdown
- fraud, sabotage, extortion or commercial espionage
- infiltration of IT systems by viruses and other forms of malicious software
- industrial action or other unavailability of key staff.

There are three key elements to BCM:

- reduction or avoidance of identified risks (on the basis that prevention is better than cure)
- planning for the recovery of business processes should a risk materialise and a business disruption occur
- transference of all or part of the risk to a third party (eg an insurer, or via outsourcing or, in government, the private finance initiative).

Insurance is an important element of planning for business continuity but should only be considered as providing compensation when other means of managing the risk have been exhausted. Within UK government insurance requires careful cost justification and approval from HM Treasury.

The BCM lifecycle consists of four distinct stages:

Stage 1 – Initiation

- sets policy for BCM
- ensures that BCM is integrated with other business and technical policies
- establishes the BCM initiative

Stage 2 – Requirements and strategy

- assesses the potential business impacts and risks
- identifies and evaluates options for reducing risk and recovering business processes and develops a cost effective BCM strategy

Stage 3 – Implementation

- establishes a programme by which business continuity will be achieved
- implements the stand-by facilities and risk reduction measures specified within the BCM strategy
- develops the requisite business recovery plans and procedures
- undertakes initial testing

Stage 4 – Operational management
- ensures that the business continuity strategy, plans and procedures continue to be tested, reviewed and maintained on an on-going basis
- puts in place suitable training and awareness programmes.

Each stage consists of one or more processes. A process model for BCM is depicted in Figure 1.

Where BCM is being introduced to an organisation for the first time this is usually in the form of a project to address stages 1, 2 and 3 of the lifecycle. However, BCM is an on-going management discipline and once implementation and initial testing have been completed the project will give way to ongoing operational management (stage 4 of the lifecycle).

Chapters 3 to 6 provide detailed descriptions of the processes and activities involved in each stage of the BCM lifecycle.

Annex A provides a listing of all activities within each process.

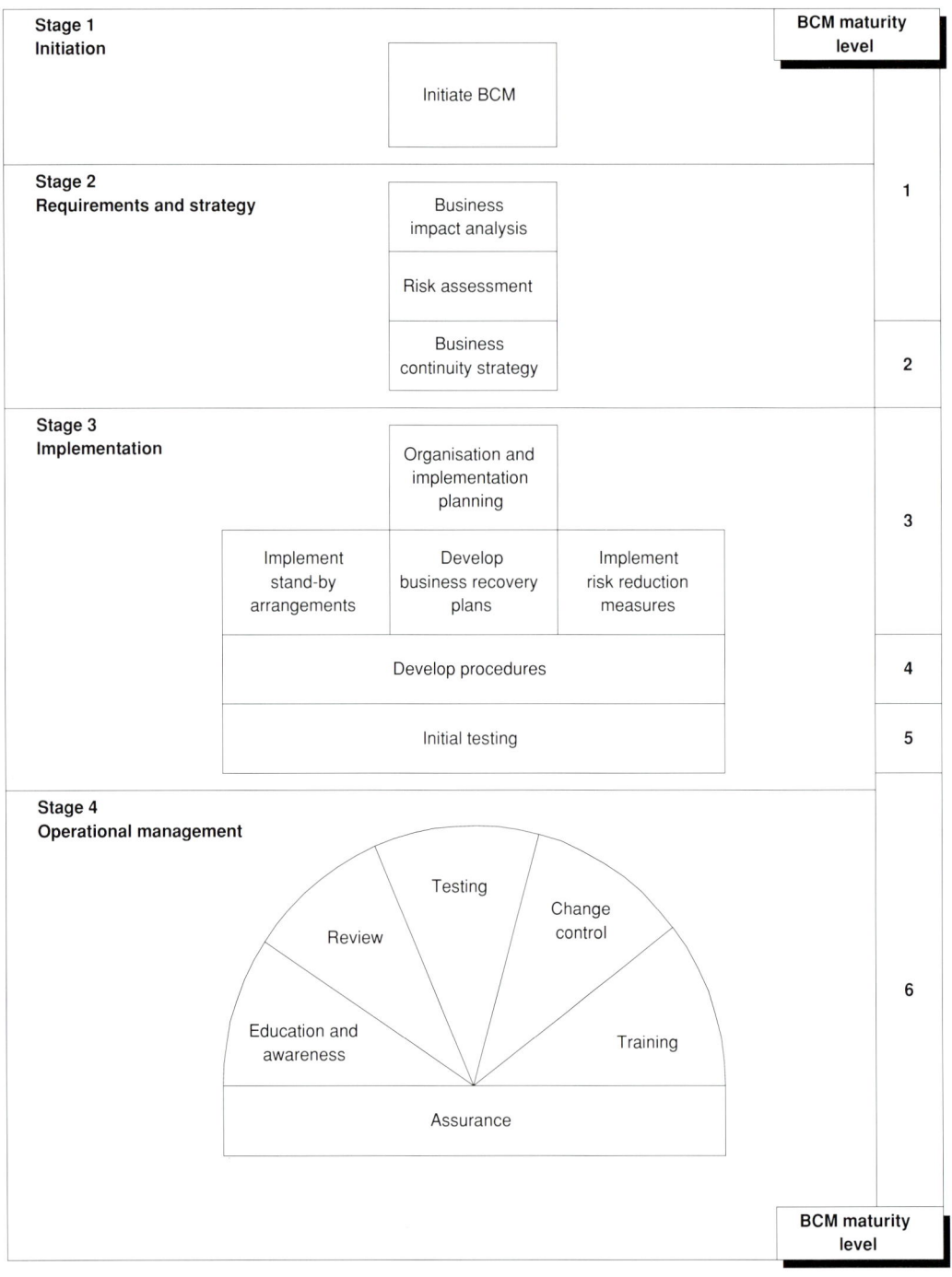

Figure 1 Business continuity management process model

3 Stage 1 of the lifecycle – Initiation

Initiation of BCM is a key process since the way in which BCM is established in an organisation influences its likely success. Senior management commitment, the correct allocation of resources and effective project management are all fundamental to the BCM initiative.

The activities to be undertaken during the initiation process depend on whether BCM is being introduced to the organisation for the first time or whether some parts of the process are already in place, for example, contingency planning for IT systems.

This chapter is written largely from the perspective of introducing BCM in a greenfield situation, usually via a BCM project. But where some BCM activities are already carried out, there is a need for overall co-ordination into a wider BCM initiative. See how the existing plan maps onto the overall requirement, modify it if necessary, and introduce the new requirements.

The initiation process consists of the following activities:

- set policy
- specify terms of reference and scope
- allocate resources
- define project organisation and control structure
- agree project and quality plans.

3.1 Set policy

BCM is concerned with the performance, and potentially the survival, of an organisation and is, therefore, a top management issue requiring significant and positive commitment from that level. The CCTA *Introduction to Business continuity management* provides guidance on how to generate awareness and commitment to BCM at senior levels.

As soon as practically possible, senior management should set policy for BCM and communicate this throughout the organisation. At the simplest level, policy could be articulated in statements in line with those recommended in the new British Standard BS7799, entitled *A Code of Practice for Information Security Management*, namely:

- a managed business continuity process will be established

- a framework of business continuity plans will be produced and maintained
- an ongoing programme of testing will be established
- business continuity plans will be updated regularly.

When the requirements analysis has been completed and a business continuity strategy established (Stage 2 of the lifecycle) additional policy decisions may be taken and communicated to staff, eg relating to:

- (contractual) arrangements with suppliers
- education and training for staff
- retention and management of critical information (documentation and electronic media).

Policy for BCM will almost certainly overlap with that in other areas and care should be taken to ensure that BCM policy is compatible with other business and technical policies.

3.2 Specify terms of reference and scope

The terms of reference for BCM usually reflect the BCM processes described in more detail in Chapters 4, 5 and 6 below. Sample terms of reference covering the entire BCM lifecycle are as follows:

- undertake a business impact analysis (to identify the potential damage or loss that may be caused to the organisation as a result of a disruption to critical business processes), identify recovery objectives and determine minimum requirements
- perform a risk assessment to determine the likelihood that a disaster or other serious incident will actually occur
- evaluate risk reduction and recovery options, select appropriate options and define a business continuity strategy
- if the business continuity strategy involves the use of third party recovery services, identify suitable vendors and evaluate and select services
- determine the command, control and communications structure necessary to control

Chapter 3
Stage 1 of the lifecycle – Initiation

business recovery activities following a major business disruption

- implement risk reduction and recovery measures
- develop a business continuity plan framework to be used as the basis for producing an integrated set of plans
- produce detailed plans and supporting procedures based on the framework describing all the actions necessary to implement stand-by arrangements and maintain business continuity
- conduct initial tests of the stand-by arrangements and business continuity plans and initiate an ongoing programme of testing
- provide initial training for managers and staff and initiate an ongoing programme of education, awareness and training
- establish review, change control, maintenance and audit procedures to ensure that the BCM strategies, plans and procedures remain up to date and workable.

Broadly, the scope of BCM is usually defined in terms of the:

- business processes to be covered and their key components such as staff, accommodation, information and systems
- degree to which external service providers should be included
- risks to be addressed.

Chapter 4 includes a description of the risks that are typically addressed by BCM. In defining the scope, the possibility of partial (as opposed to total) disasters should not be overlooked. In fact, incidents that disable part of a business process (eg a fire on one floor of a building) are much more common than total destruction but often require separate recovery solutions.

3.3 Allocate resources Having set business continuity policy and defined the terms of reference and scope, senior management will need to allocate suitable financial and manpower resources.

The overall financial and manpower commitment required for BCM will not become apparent until a business continuity strategy has been developed. It should, however, be at a level agreed by management as being commensurate with the potential business impacts and perceived risks. The immediate resourcing concern therefore relates to the costs involved in undertaking the requirements analysis and developing a business continuity strategy (Stage 2 of the lifecycle).

Carrying out the requirements analysis and developing a business continuity strategy involves management and staff time and, possibly, training or use of experienced external consultancy support. Stage 2 of the lifecycle is primarily an information gathering and analysis exercise and the effort involved is determined by the number of managers and staff who need to be consulted and the time required for the analysis and quality review of deliverables. This in turn depends on the scope of the exercise in terms of the number of business processes and the risks to be covered.

The elapsed time for Stage 2 will typically be one to six months depending on its scope.

Chapter 7 describes the skills and techniques required for BCM.

3.4 Define project organisation and control structure

Like all important projects, a BCM project needs to be well organised and controlled.

Other CCTA volumes, such as the PRINCE (PRojects In Controlled Environments) Manuals and the *PRINCE User's Guide to CRAMM*, provide guidance on project organisation and control.

A typical project organisation for BCM would include:

- assignment of overall responsibility for the project, and for accepting the deliverables, to a member of the Management Board

- the establishment of a steering committee, or PRINCE Project Board, to direct the project, ensure that resources are made available, and that deliverables are quality assured, and advise the Management Board on the acceptability of the deliverables

- the appointment of a project manager to control the day-to-day running of the project and a project team to undertake many of the project activities

- the establishment of working groups to undertake some of the project activities that require specialist expertise, for example, implementation of stand-by arrangements, production of detailed procedures for the recovery of systems and data.

A BCM project would typically be controlled by:

- producing and maintaining a Project Initiation Document (PID) which describes the terms of reference and scope, activities and deliverables, the way in which the project is organised and controlled, the project plans, quality plans, assumptions and risks
- regular monitoring of progress against the project and quality plans
- a defined quality review process which involves formal acceptance of all deliverables
- regular progress reports to the Management Board.

3.5 Agree project and quality plans

Project plans for BCM typically show:

- start dates, end dates and resources and their responsibilities allocated to each stage, process and, where appropriate, activity
- dates for the production of draft and final deliverables
- important dependencies
- dates for quality review meetings, Project Board meetings and presentations to the Management Board.

A BCM quality plan includes:

- a *product description* for each deliverable outlining the proposed contents
- criteria by which the quality of each deliverable is to be judged
- a description of the person responsible for undertaking quality reviews of each deliverable.

Annex B includes sample product descriptions and quality criteria for key BCM deliverables.

IT Infrastructure Library
A Guide to Business Continuity Management

4 Stage 2 of the lifecycle – Requirements and strategy

At this stage in BCM the organisation assesses its business requirements and risks and decides on the optimum approach to managing business continuity. It is a critical stage in the BCM lifecycle since decisions taken here determine how well the organisation will actually survive a disaster and the costs it will incur on BCM. Errors or omissions at this stage will have serious implications at later stages in the lifecycle.

The requirements analysis and strategy definition stage consists of the following processes:

- perform business impact analysis
- perform risk assessment
- develop business continuity strategy.

The activities within each process are described in the following sections.

4.1 Business impact analysis

A key driver in determining BCM requirements is 'how much the organisation stands to lose' as a result of a disaster or other incident and how quickly these losses would materialise. This can be assessed through a business impact analysis.

The purpose of a business impact analysis is to identify:

- critical business processes
- the potential damage or loss that may be caused to the organisation as a result of a disruption to critical business processes.

The business impact analysis also identifies:

- the form that the damage or loss may take, eg lost income, additional costs, loss of goodwill
- how the degree of damage or loss is likely to escalate after an incident
- the minimum staffing, facilities and services necessary to enable business processes to continue operating at a minimum acceptable level
- the time within which minimum levels of staffing, facilities and services should be recovered

- the time within which business processes and all supporting staff, facilities and services should be fully recovered.

The business impact analysis process consists of the following activities:

- identify business processes
- define impact scenarios
- measure potential business impacts
- define business recovery objectives
- assess minimum requirements.

Identify business processes

A business process is a group of business activities undertaken by an organisation in pursuit of a common goal. Typical business processes include:

- marketing products and services
- receiving orders
- manufacturing products
- selling products
- delivering services
- distributing products
- invoicing for services
- accounting for money received.

A business process may be undertaken by a single business function (eg a department or division) or several business functions working together. A business process will usually depend on several business support functions, eg IT, Personnel, Office Services.

Business processes rarely operate in isolation and are becoming increasingly integrated as technology develops.

Since BCM is focused on maintaining the continuity of critical business processes, an important first step is to identify, and where necessary group together, business processes for the purpose of the business impact analysis. A separate business impact analysis will be carried out for each business process or group of processes.

Chapter 4
Stage 2 of the lifecycle – Requirements and strategy

The following sources can be useful starting points for identifying business processes:

- strategic or business planning documents
- output from business process re-engineering initiatives
- organisational information models.

In the absence of any source information on business processes, the process managers should be requested to produce an initial list of those they manage.

Having identified business processes, the next step is to decide which processes or groups of processes should be included in the business impact analysis. This decision is influenced by:

- the scope of the analysis, ie whether all processes are included, whether the purpose is a high level scoping study or a full study etc
- management's initial perception of the critical business processes
- the degree of integration and interdependence between business processes.

It should be remembered that the purpose of the business impact analysis is to assess the impacts that could result from disruption to business processes. Where business processes are closely integrated or highly dependent on each other and the potential impacts from disruption are similar, then these processes can be considered together for the purpose of the business impact analysis.

Example:
Consider time-sensitive products such as newspapers and magazines where the processes of writing editorial copy, incorporating advertisements, production (including reprographics and printing) and distribution are all closely integrated.

A disruption to any of these processes could cause the product to be late on sale with a resulting impact of lost circulation and advertising revenue and, possibly, longer-term loss of market share.

Little would be gained by undertaking a business impact analysis separately for each of the above processes. In fact, if they are considered in isolation from each other there is a risk that inconsistent conclusions will be drawn.

For the purpose of a business impact analysis, the processes should be considered together (perhaps described as 'deliver product to point of sale') with a focus on assessing the losses that could result from the product being late on sale.

In deciding whether or not to group business processes together it should be remembered that a separate business impact analysis will be required for each process or group of processes. Where there is some debate, it is advisable to err on the side of grouping the processes. It soon becomes apparent during the analysis if particular processes need to be considered separately from the group.

Define impact scenarios

Potential business impacts are measured for each process (or group of processes) against defined impact scenarios for the process. In the example given above the impact scenario was the *product is late on sale*.

Examples of other possible impact scenarios are as follows:

- for the service delivery process – services cannot be provided to customers
- for the receipt of orders process – orders cannot be processed
- for the invoicing for services process – invoices are delayed.

Each impact scenario needs to be investigated in relation to a range of timescales in order to see how the potential impacts will change with time. For example, it may be necessary to know the potential impact if orders cannot be processed for one day, two days, one week, two weeks and one month. The period within the month or year may also have a significant bearing on the potential impact.

The impact scenarios and the timescales to be investigated for each process will depend on the risks included within the scope of the exercise. For example:

- if the concern is with physical disasters such as fire, flood and terrorism the potential disruption could last for many months and it would be important to know how the impact would grow over many months

Chapter 4
Stage 2 of the lifecycle – Requirements and strategy

- if the concern is with technical failures then it may be reasonable to assume that the disruption would be limited to one to two weeks.

Measuring potential impacts against some or all of the following time periods will usually give a good indication of how impacts will change with time:

- less than 15 minutes
- 1 hour
- 3 hours
- 12 hours
- 1 day
- 2 days
- 1 week
- 2 weeks
- 1 month
- 2 months and over.

The impact analysis will concentrate on those scenarios where the impact is likely to be greatest and the time periods used should, as much as possible, reflect the situation that is likely to occur in practice.

As far as possible, impact scenarios and time periods should be identified for each process (or group of processes) before discussions/interviews to measure the potential business impacts are held with management.

Measure potential business impacts

Having identified impact scenarios, business impacts are usually measured by interviewing managers responsible for the business processes to assess the potential scale of the impact. In some cases records of previous incidents may prove useful, eg records showing how revenue dropped during a contractor's industrial dispute may give some indication of the impacts that might result from a future disruption.

Potential business impacts for each business process should be measured for each impact scenario and time period.

Measurements of business impacts fall into two categories, hard (financial) or soft (non-financial). Hard impacts are quantifiable in pounds sterling, dollars or other denominations whilst soft impacts cannot be quantified in financial terms.

Typical hard and soft impacts are described below:

Hard impacts

- financial loss, eg through loss of an asset that needs to be re-purchased
- reduced income
- increased cost of working, eg as a result of hiring additional temporary staff
- financial penalties, eg as a result of failing to deliver agreed service levels or failing to meet statutory obligations.

Soft impacts

- loss of goodwill
- loss of credibility
- political, corporate or personal embarrassment
- breach of the law
- risk to personal safety
- loss of operational capability, for example in a command and control environment.

Hard impacts provide useful information on which to base a cost justification of business continuity measures and, wherever possible, hard impacts should be assessed. Most financial impacts can be reduced down to one or more of the four hard impacts described above. For example, a long-term loss of market share would result in reduced income and possibly an increased cost of working through the loss of economies of scale or difficulty in raising capital.

In assessing hard impacts, the following points should be remembered:

- the financial impact relating to the impact scenario is the *marginal* (net) financial impact, ie if income reduces by £1 million but costs reduce by £400,000 (perhaps through savings on raw materials), the marginal financial impact is £600,000
- if the impact scenario can result in different types of financial impact, eg lost income,

Chapter 4
Stage 2 of the lifecycle – Requirements and strategy

additional cost of working, financial penalties, these should be recorded separately and then combined into an assessment of the overall financial impact

- where insurance cover is in place to protect against additional cost of working, loss of profit etc then details of the risks covered, level of cover provided, any excess and the annual premiums should be recorded separately but should not, at this stage, be used to reduce the potential financial impact which has been measured for the scenario.

It may be possible to measure some of the soft impacts described above in financial terms. However, this is often highly subjective and should be avoided unless there is reasonable confidence in the financial values used. Soft impacts should, however, always be documented since they will provide added justification to any business case for business continuity measures. Some risk assessment methods such as the CCTA Risk Analysis and Management Method (CRAMM) include guidelines and metrics which are useful for recording and comparing both soft and hard impacts.

It is often useful to produce a graphical representation of how business impacts vary with length of disruption as illustrated in Figure 2.

Define business recovery objectives

Business recovery objectives are statements relating to the need to continue business processes. They are derived from the measurement of potential business impacts and describe a minimum acceptable level of operation for each business process.

Business recovery objectives take a similar form to impact scenarios, but are qualified by a time objective, eg:

- product X must be no more than **three days** late on sale

- a skeleton customer services operation must be resumed within **twelve hours** and a full service within **one week**

- order processing must be resumed within **two days**

- invoicing must be resumed within **two weeks** for major accounts and within **four weeks** for all other accounts.

Recovery objectives should be discussed and agreed with the managers responsible for the business processes in the light of findings from the measurement of potential business impacts.

The business recovery objectives (as stated at this stage) cannot always be met. It may for example prove too expensive to provide the necessary stand-by arrangements. The recovery objectives will, however, form the starting point from which different recovery options can be evaluated.

Assess minimum requirements

All business processes depend to some degree on people, assets and services. In many cases, business processes can be re-established without the full complement of staff, systems and other assets and services. Often the 80/20 rule will apply.

Once business recovery objectives have been defined, the final activity during the business impact analysis process is to assess the minimum requirements for people, assets and services that will enable the objectives to be met.

Most commonly, this involves assessing the minimum requirements for:

- computer networks
- staff and accommodation
- computer systems and data
- voice, facsimile and other forms of communications
- paper records
- other assets and services.

Chapter 4
Stage 2 of the lifecycle – Requirements and strategy

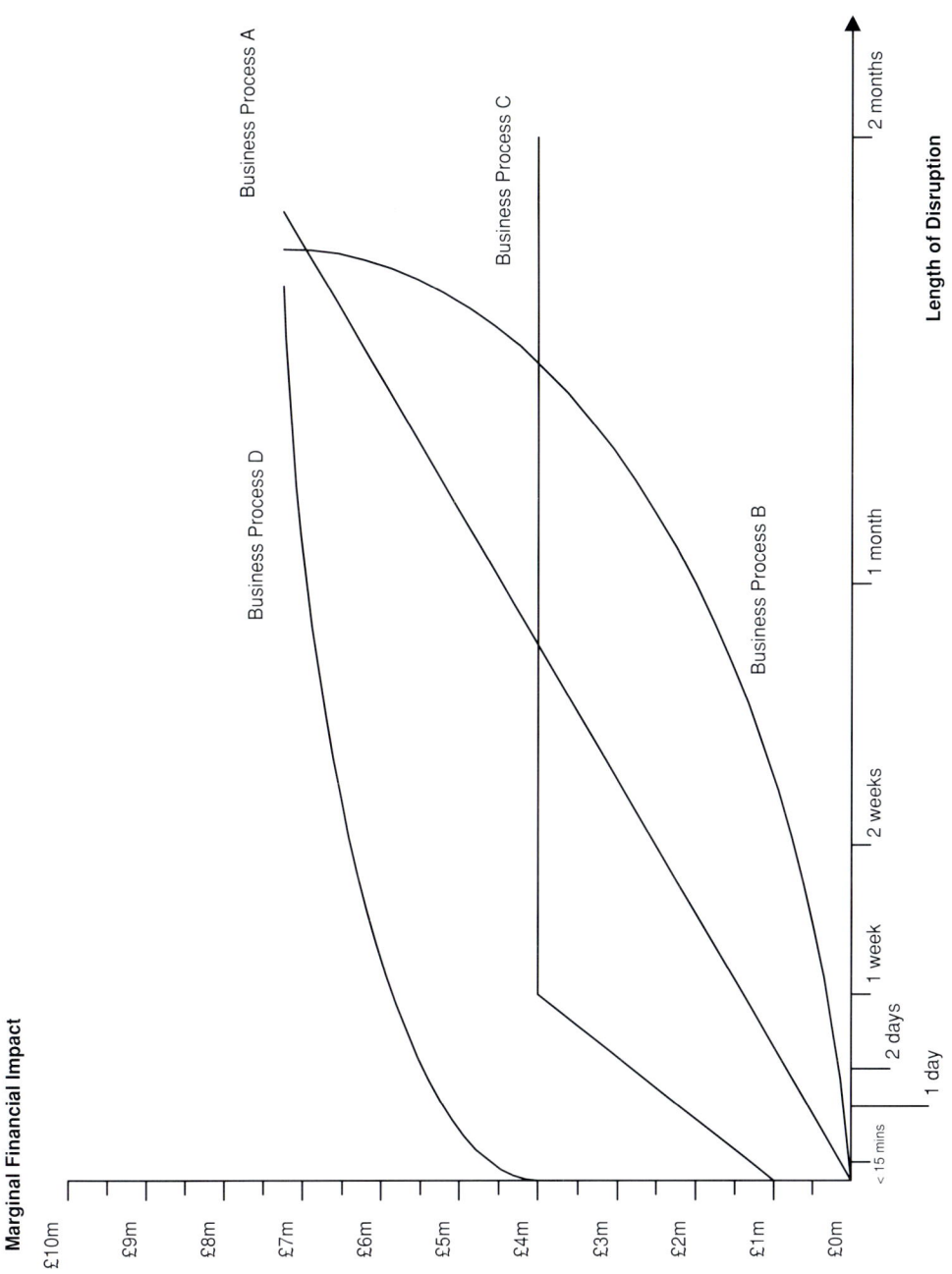

Figure 2 Graphical representation of business impacts

Figure 3 shows a sample form for recording details of minimum requirements for each business process. The level of detail indicated on the form should, in most situations, be sufficient to enable business recovery options to be identified and evaluated. It is not the intention of the form as shown to gather full configuration details for computer systems and networks.

Where the computer systems environment is particularly complex or where there is a need to record detailed configuration information (eg for a specific IT contingency planning exercise) a separate form such as that shown in Figure 4 can be used.

Having recorded minimum requirements for each business process it is often useful to consolidate the information across all processes. Figure 5 provides an example of how consolidated requirements can be presented for people, assets and services.

Information of the type shown on Figures 3, 4 and 5 together provides the specifications against which recovery options can be identified and evaluated. All the forms can be taken and used directly or amended to meet the specific requirements of the exercise.

CRAMM Version 3 provides automated support for recording and presenting business impact assessments, recovery objectives and recovery requirements.

4.2 Risk assessment

The second key driver in determining BCM requirements is 'the likelihood that a disaster or other serious incident will actually occur'. This is a function of the level of threat and the extent of the organisation's vulnerability to each threat.

The risk assessment process consists of the following activities:

- identify risks
- assess threat and vulnerability levels
- assess levels of risk.

Chapter 4
Stage 2 of the lifecycle – Requirements and strategy

Name of business process	
1 Normal staff numbers	
2 Minimum staff numbers (core team size)	
3 Time within which the core team must be recovered	
4 Maximum time for which the business process can operate with only a core team	
5 Description of computer systems normally used by the business process. Include system name (eg accounts), hardware used (eg IBM AS400) and the number of machines/terminals, printers used	
6 Description of the minimum computer systems required to support the core team. This will be a subset of the description given in 5	
7 Decription of any computer networking requirements to support the core team. Describe the number of network access points required for the computer systems described in 6	
8 Number of telephones, fax machines and other communications services required by the core team	
9 Description of any critical paper records necessary to support the core team	
10 Other services or assets required by the core team. List any other assets or services that are critical to the core team, eg modems for access to external services, photocopiers	

Figure 3 Sample form for recording minimum requirements

IT Infrastructure Library
A Guide to Business Continuity Management

Name of Business Process						Computer Services				
Team		Time to recover					Time to recover		Support Staff Required	
Description	Number	Days/Hours	Description	Number	Service Levels	Other Requirements/Comments		Description	Number	
(Description of Users)	(Insert minimum acceptable number of Users)	(Insert the recovery time required)	(Describe the minimum computer assets and services required by users within the time stated)	(Insert the number of assets/services required within the time)	(Describe any required service levels within the time, eg response times)	(Give any other requirements or comments)		(Insert a description of the support staff required to enable users to be recovered within the time)	(Insert the number of support staff required)	
Team A (Core)	20	12 hours	Sales Workstations	20		minimum 486/50				
			Sales Servers	2						
			Bridge	1				Network Implementation Team	3	
			X.25 Switch	1						
			Mega Stream A	1		2 Mbps		System Administrator	1	
			Telesales S/W	20		1 copy per workstation				
			etc							
Team B	50	2 Days	Sales Workstations	50		minimum 486/66				
			Sales Servers	4						
			Bridge	2		1 bridge shared with Team A. Other bridge dedicated to Team B		Network Implementation Team	3	
			X.25 Switch	1		Shared with Team A		System Administrator	1	
			Mega Stream B	1		8 Mbps				
			Telesales S/W	50		1 copy per workstation				

Figure 4 Sample form for recording minimum requirements for computer systems and networks

Chapter 4
Stage 2 of the lifecycle – Requirements and strategy

Description of Assets or Services	Team Description	Recover Within										
		<15 mins	1 hour	3 hours	12 hours	1 day	2 days	1 week	2 weeks	1 month	2 months & Over
		Insert the numbers of people, assets or services for each time period									
Accomm-odation (people)	Team A			20							
	Team B					50	30	50	50		
	Team C			10					20		
Total				30		50	30	50	70		
Sales Workstations	Team A				20		50				
	Team B				10		30				
	Team C				30						
Total					30		80				
Sales Servers	Team A						4				
	Team B										
	Team C						2				
Total							6				

Figure 5 Consolidated recovery requirements for people, assets and services

IT Infrastructure Library
A Guide to Business Continuity Management

Identify risks

Risks relate to particular components of the business process. For example an organisation might decide that the impact scenario, *services cannot be provided to customers for X hours* could result from:

- disaster or denial of access to location A (eg where critical computer systems are located) which might be owned by an external service provider

- disaster or denial of access to location B (eg where the customer services function is located)

- loss of power or telecommunications services to either site

- failure of a critical computer system

- industrial action by customer services staff, and so on.

Figure 6 provides a list of typical risks to continuous business processing.

Assess threat and vulnerability levels

A threat assessment is a measure of 'the likelihood that a disaster or other serious incident will actually be initiated'. In the case of a deliberate threat, a high threat assessment indicates a high likelihood that an attack will be made. A high threat does not indicate whether or not the attack is likely to succeed – this depends on the extent of the organisation's vulnerability to the threat.

For accidental threats, a high threat assessment indicates a high probability that an incident will be initiated, eg a computer failure, human error. Again, this only results in problems for the organisation if it is vulnerable to such an incident.

Threats and vulnerabilities are two separate, but related, components of risk and need to be understood, if an effective business continuity strategy is to be developed. The threat assessment and vulnerability assessment together give a measure of the likelihood of successful attack or the likelihood of an incident occurring.

Example
An organisation performing experiments on live animals might be considered to be under a high threat of attack from animal rights groups. If the site is well protected physically then the vulnerability to an external attack would be considered to be low. The likelihood of a

Chapter 4
Stage 2 of the lifecycle – Requirements and strategy

Risk	Threat sources	Threat factors	Vulnerability factors
1 Damage or denial of access to premises	Accidental fire	Internal policies and procedures (eg no smoking, clean desk)	Single point of failure Weak security procedures
	Arson and vandalism	Location	Single point of failure Weak security procedures
	Flood	Location	Single point of failure
	Aircraft impact	Location	Single point of failure
	Weather damage eg hurricane	Location	Single point of failure
	Environmental disaster	Location	Single point of failure
	Terrorist attack	Nature of business conducted at premises or in close proximity	Single point of failure Weak environmental policies and procedures
	Sabotage	Disgruntled staff	Single point of failure Weak personnel procedures
2 Loss of IT systems/networks PABXs, ACDs etc	All of the above	As above	As above
	Catastrophic failure	Old, untested or unreliable equipment	Poor management procedures Lack of resilience
	Electrical damage, eg lightning	Location	Poor lightning protection measures
	Poor quality software	Untrained or demotivated personnel	Poor development or change control procedures
3 Loss of data	Technical failure	Unreliable equipment or software	Lack of resilience Poor back-up procedures
	Human error	Poor training, demotivated staff	Poor management procedures Poor back-up procedures
	Viruses or other malicious software	High volumes of software and data coming in from external sources	Weak policies and procedures Poor back-up procedures

Figure 6 Typical risks

IT Infrastructure Library
A Guide to Business Continuity Management

Risk	Threat sources	Threat factors	Vulnerability factors
4 Loss of network services (eg services provided by BT, Mercury)	Damage, denial of access to premises of network service providers.	As above in 1	As above in 1
	Loss of service provider's IT systems/networks	As above in 2	As above in 2
	Loss of service provider's data	As above in 3	As above in 3
	Failure of the service providers	As below in 6	As below in 6
5 Unavailability of key staff	Industrial action	Poor industrial relations	Over-dependence on key staff
	Resignation	Shortage of specialist skills	Over-dependence on key staff
	Sickness/injury	Working environment epidemics	Over-dependence on key staff
	Transport difficulties	Location	Over-dependence on key staff
6 Failure of service providers	Commercial failure, eg insolvency	Nature of business, eg capital intensive, highly competitive. Quality and experience of management.	Over-dependence on key suppliers
	Unavailability of service providers' staff	As in 5 above	Over-dependence on key suppliers
	Failure to meet contracted service levels	No prior experience on providing required service levels/poor maintenance	Over-dependence on key suppliers
7 Loss of critical paper records	As in 1 above	As in 1 above	As in 1 above Poor back-up procedures
8 Loss of power	Deliberate or accidental damage to the grid	Location	Single point of failure
	Unavailability of staff, eg industrial action by providers' staff	As in 5 above	Lack of emergency power facilities

Figure 6 (*continued*) Typical risks

successful external attack would therefore be considered to be medium or low.

However, if no suitable background checks and procedures for supervision of staff were in place, the organisation would be highly vulnerable to an internal act of sabotage. The likelihood of a successful internal attack would, therefore, be considered to be high.

Where reliable statistical information on the likelihood of incidents is available this should always be used since it enables a quantitative cost benefit analysis to be carried out for potential risk reduction or recovery options. However, suitable statistical information is very rare, tending to exist only for the threat of technical failure where previous reliability figures may be available. In the absence of quantitative risk assessment information, the alternative approach is to look for factors that might indicate particular levels of threat or expose significant vulnerabilities.

The level of threat will depend on factors such as:

- likely motivation, capability and resources for deliberate incidents
- for accidental incidents, the organisation's location, environment, and the quality of its internal systems and procedures.

Business processes are highly vulnerable where there are critical single points of failure, typical examples of which are:

- a concentration of high proportions of staff, systems, records and other critical assets in a single geographic location
- a reliance on individual service providers
- dependence on individuals or small groups of people for critical business activities
- communications networks with no inbuilt resilience.

Figure 6 lists factors to be considered when assessing levels of threat or vulnerability. Factors relating to identified threats and vulnerabilities should be recorded for later use during the business continuity strategy process.

IT Infrastructure Library
A Guide to Business Continuity Management

Assess levels of risk

The overall risk to an organisation is a function of:

- *how much the organisation stands to lose* as a result of a disaster or other incident, and as measured by the impact analysis

- *the likelihood that a disaster or other serious incident will actually occur*, as measured during the assessment of threats and vulnerabilities.

If quantitative assessments are available for both of these then a quantitative measurement of risk can be made. Otherwise, a qualitative description of, say, low, medium or high risks should be used.

Information gathered during the risk assessment is used during the business continuity strategy process to:

- assist with the identification of risk reduction options to address known vulnerabilities

- inform the evaluation of risk reduction and recovery options.

Further guidance on how to measure business impacts and risks can be found in the CCTA Management of Risk Library and in the CCTA Risk Analysis and Management Method (CRAMM).

4.3 Business continuity strategy

The business continuity strategy defines how the continuity of business processes is to be maintained in the event of a disaster or other serious incident. The strategy covers both risk reduction and recovery.

Information gathered during the business impact analysis process, on recovery objectives and the minimum staffing, facilities and services necessary to enable business processes to continue operating at a minimum acceptable level, is used to specify and identify recovery and risk reduction options. Information gathered on potential business impacts and the risk assessment is used during the evaluation of options.

The business continuity strategy process consists of the following activities:

- identify and evaluate recovery options
- identify and evaluate risk reduction options
- define overall strategy.

Identify and evaluate recovery options	Recovery options should be identified that can provide the minimum requirements to enable business processes to continue operating at a minimum acceptable level, and broadly satisfy the recovery objectives. An integrated set of recovery options is usually required to support critical business processes. Typically, this set includes options for recovery of:

- people and accommodation
- IT systems, networks and data
- critical services such as power, telecommunications and post
- critical assets such as paper records, reference material and post.

Depending upon the recovery objectives, it may be necessary to consider different options for short-term and long-term recovery. Where business processes are highly dependent on external service providers, recovery options need to be considered that address the risk of failure by service providers.

Figure 7 shows typical recovery options. This list should not be considered to be exhaustive but it provides a good starting point for the identification of options.

An option should not necessarily be disregarded if recovery objectives cannot be met through use of the option. In the absence of other suitable cost effective options there may be no other choice than to accept a relaxation in recovery objectives.

The important factors in undertaking a financial evaluation of recovery options are as follows:

- the reduction in potential impact that will result from implementing the option
- the cost of setting up, maintaining and testing the option – eg staff resources, capital expenditure, contract premiums, training, consultancy
- the cost of invoking the option in the event of an incident or disaster, eg hiring temporary staff, invocation fees for commercial recovery services – these may be recoverable against insurance

- the likelihood that an incident or disaster will actually occur and the consequences if it does.

A simple concept for financial evaluation of options is that of Annual Loss Expectancy (ALE).

The US Federal Information Processing Standard (FIPS) Publication No. 65 contains a detailed description of the process.

ALE is a measure of the annual loss that can be expected from an incident or disaster and is calculated as follows:

ALE = Potential Impact (Loss) X Likelihood of the
 from an incident   incident occurring

Using the ALE approach, an option is said to be justified if it produces a reduction in ALE that is greater than the (annual) cost of the option. Annex D contains an example of how ALE can be applied.

The major difficulty with ALE-based evaluations is that they rely on there being hard (financial) measurements of potential impact and, critically, rely on a largely unknown factor, the likelihood of an incident occurring. Actuarial information on the likelihood of incidents is scarce and, where it is available, difficult to interpret in relation to specific circumstances.

The ALE approach can be useful, in certain circumstances, for undertaking a financial evaluation of options. However, in coming to a conclusion on the optimum approach to take, the following should also be considered:

- additional *soft* benefits that would be provided by the option, eg retaining goodwill
- whether the level of threat is perceived to be low, medium or high
- whether vulnerabilities can be reduced by other means, eg by improving risk reduction measures
- the degree of confidence in the approach taken, ie will it work as anticipated
- the stability provided by the option, eg if an option involves providing stand-by facilities at other vacant accommodation controlled by the organisation, is there a risk that the vacant accommodation could be disposed of?

Chapter 4
Stage 2 of the lifecycle – Requirements and strategy

Risk	Solutions	Typical recovery options	Comments
Loss or denial of access to accommodation	Identify and provide for alternative accommodation. Recovery will be quicker if the accommodation has been pre-equipped with the appropriate power, telephone and computer network infrastructure	1 identify and monitor the availability of suitable stand-by accommodation, either within the organisation or outside.	Accommodation may be freed up but will probably need to be equipped before it can be used
		2. Dedicated stand-by accommodation within the organisation/group	Under the control of the organisation, can be equipped as required in advance
		3. Commercial recovery service	
		a Mobile accommodation brought in	Requires suitable access and siting
		b Accommodation provided at vendor's premises	Staff need to travel to vendor's premises
		4 Stand-by agreement with a third party, eg sister company, supplier	Third party also impacted
		5 Staff to work from home	Communications difficulties. Likely to be feasible for short periods only
		6 Resilient business process, eg by distributing key staff across several sites	Can be expensive

Figure 7 Typical recovery options

Risk	Solutions	Typical recovery options	Comments
Loss or catastrophic failure of computer hardware	Identify and provide for replacement hardware that could be obtained and commissioned at short notice	1 Use hardware from less critical business procedures	Other business processes may be impacted
	Recovery will be quicker if the replacement hardware is preconfigured with the appropriate software and peripheral hardware and quicker still if copies of data are pre-loaded and updated regularly	2. Use development test machines or spare capacity on other systems	Other business processes may be impacted
		3 Dedicated in-house contingency equipment	Expensive option
		4 Commercial recovery service	
	Ultimately, if data is replicated to stand-by machines in real time (possible with options 1, 2, 3, 4b, 5 and 7) then amost instantaneous recovery may be possible	*a Mobile service brought in*	Requires suitable access and siting
		b Service established at vendor's premises	Networking required to connect to users, or relocation of users required
		c Call-off arrangement for delivery of PC/mid-range systems	Can be expensive for large volumes
		5 Stand-by arrangement with a third party, eg sister company	Significant effort required to maintain compatibility. Third party also impacted
		6 Rush orders placed immediately post disaster	Risk that sufficient equipment will not be obtained in order to meet recovery objectives
		7 Resilient, distributed system architecture	Becoming more feasible as technology develops
		8 Fall-back to a manual process until replacement hardware can be procured and installed	Risk that recovery objectives will not be achieved with the manual process

Figure 7 (*continued*) Typical recovery options

Risk	Solutions	Typical recovery options	Comments
Catastrophic failure of computer software	Facilities to enable business processes to fall-back to alternative ways of operating	1 Back-ups of earlier working version	Back-up copies should be protected against malicious damage
		2 Fall-back to a manual process until fixes can be made	Risk reduction measures such as rigorous testing and phased implementation of new software are critical
Technical failure of computer systems	Provide for rapid fault fixing or, where non-stop operation is required, provide fault tolerant architectures	1 On-site or rapid response support team with stocks of emergency spares and appropriate software expertise	Risk that recovery objectives may not be achieved. Risk that emergency fixes to software might further compromise business continuity or security
		2 Fault tolerant architectures, eg multiple processors and/or disks	Expensive option, but provides non-stop operation
		3 Back-up copies of software	Back-up copies should be protected against malicious damage
Loss of data	Back-ups taken at a frequency which reflects the potential business impact from loss of data. Back-ups should be protected and stored well away from the 'live' versions	1 Removable media, eg tape, diskette, cartridge, CD-ROM	Time required to re-load data. Data not fully up-to-date
		2 Remote journalling/ electronic vaulting	Can be expensive, but allows rapid recovery
		3 Real-time disk mirroring	Expensive option, limits on distance between disks, but can provide for almost instantaneous recovery

Figure 7 (*continued*) Typical recovery options

IT Infrastructure Library
A Guide to Business Continuity Management

Risk	Solutions	Typical recovery options	Comments
Loss of network services	Resilient network design or alternative services	1 Resilient network design with dynamic alternative routing	Can only be controlled on private networks
		2 Alternative cable routes	
		3 Alternative service access points and switch nodes	
		4 Alternative access methods, eg switched or wireless as a fall-back to permanent connections	
		5 Virtual Private Networks with contracted service levels	Passes some of the risk to the service provider
Loss of PABX or Automatic Call Distribution (ACD) systems	Identify and provide for replacement equipment	1 Commercial recovery service, eg replacement PABX on a trailer	Requires access and siting. Cabling takes time. Wireless versions becoming available
Unavailability of key staff	Avoid over-dependence on key individuals and identify and provide for alternative staff	1 Cross-discipline training	Must be kept up-to-date
		2 Outsourcing	May introduce other risks
		3 Documentation of all key activities	May be difficult to maintain
		4 Identifying sources of temporary staff	May be difficult to identify appropriate technical staff
Failure of service providers	Avoid over-dependence on key suppliers and identify and provide for alternatives	1 Active supplier management	Encourage service providers to introduce their own business continuity and security initiatives
		2 Identify alternative suppliers capable of taking over the work at short notice	May not be feasible within the required time
		3 Limit the amount of business given to any one supplier	May not be the most cost-effective approach

Figure 7 (*continued*) Typical recovery options

Chapter 4
Stage 2 of the lifecycle – Requirements and strategy

Risk	Solutions	Typical recovery options	Comments
Loss of critical paper records	Ensure alternative sources of the information are available	1 Duplication and off-site storage	Can be expensive
		2 Fiche or document image processing	Can be expensive or functionally difficult
		3 Request suppliers/third parties to retain duplicate data	Requires consideration of security issues
Loss of power	Ensure alternative sources of power	1 Back-up generators for critical services, eg lighting, key systems	Uninterruptible power supply may be required to protect data
		2 Alternative cable routes to the substations	May be difficult or very expensive to achieve
		3 Connection to alternative substations	Expensive, and may be difficult to achieve

Figure 7 (*continued*) Typical recovery options

IT Infrastructure Library
A Guide to Business Continuity Management

- compatibility of the option with future business and technical strategies within the organisation

- any organisational implications that might result from introducing the option, eg by taking staff resources from other key activities.

Care should also be taken to ensure that the introduction of an option to address one particular risk does not increase the risks in other areas.

Where insurance against particular risks is in place, or is available to the organisation (some organisations self-insure), this needs to be taken into account during analysis of options. However, care should be taken to avoid overstating the value of insurance – loss adjusters will attempt to reduce the claim and payment may take some time. Insurance is unlikely to compensate fully for long-term or soft business impacts.

Identify and evaluate risk reduction options

Effective BCM requires a suitable balance between risk reduction and recovery mechanisms. In theory, where very high levels of physical protection are provided for sites, less emphasis may be placed on recovery measures and vice versa. In practice, over reliance on one approach to the exclusion of the other is dangerous and should be avoided.

Risk reduction measures should, for example, include:

- improvements in resilience of business functions and processes by eliminating single points of failure

- consider limiting the amount of business given to any one provider of external services

- building fault tolerance and resilience into IT systems and networks

- implementing additional security such as access control or CCTV to deter or detect unauthorised access or deliberate physical attacks

- providing additional controls to detect local incidents such as fire and flood before serious damage occurs

- improving procedures to reduce the likelihood of errors or failures, eg project management, structured systems design, configuration management, change control, incident reporting, escalation procedures.

Chapter 4
Stage 2 of the lifecycle – Requirements and strategy

Risk reduction options	Typical risk reduction measures
Control over physical access to sites, buildings and rooms	Secure site layout Secure building design Building and room entry control Secure external doors Secure external windows CCTV and intruder detection devices Perimeter fencing Security lighting Control of visitors Guards and patrols
Fire protection	Fire detection and alarms Extinguishers and fire suppressant systems No smoking policy Valid fire certificate Non-combustible building designs and building contents
Flood protection	Secure siting of critical assets Moisture detection and alarms
Bomb protection	Secure site layout, secure building design, building and room entry control, control of visitors, control of deliveries, detection procedures and equipment
Protection of incoming services	Physical protection of power, telephone and data network cabling and equipment
Protection of critical electronics and paper media	Control over physical access as described above Fire and flood protection as described above Secure storage facilities, eg safes
Virus protection	Use of virus detection software

Figure 8 Typical risk reduction measures

Figure 8 describes some typical risk reduction measures.

Justification for risk reduction measures is likely to depend on more than just business continuity considerations. Physical and environmental security measures may, for example, also be required to:

- protect against theft, vandalism or espionage
- comply with Health and Safety legislation
- provide safe and secure working conditions.

In most cases, organisations will already have some risk reduction measures in place – the question for BCM therefore becomes one of whether improved or additional measures are required in the light of the risk assessment.

Suitable options need to be evaluated against identified threats and vulnerabilities from the risk assessment. Risk assessment methods that also address the management of risk (such as CRAMM) assist with the identification and evaluation of both risk reduction and business recovery options.

The business continuity strategy is determined by selecting a suitable balance of risk reduction and business recovery options to minimise the risks and meet the business recovery objectives.

Define overall strategy	If expenditure can be delayed until a disruption occurs, whilst still achieving business recovery within an acceptable time, this is likely to be the most attractive option because:

- the disruption may never occur
- where insurance is in place, additional costs incurred after the disruption occurs may be recoverable
- any costs incurred in advance will not be recoverable.

Once a balanced and integrated set of options has been identified these should be documented and agreed before moving onto Stage 3 – Implementation.

Annex B includes an outline product description and quality criteria for a business continuity strategy report.

5 Stage 3 of the lifecycle – Implementation

Once the business continuity strategy has been defined and agreed, the BCM lifecycle moves into the implementation stage. This stage involves implementation of stand-by and risk reduction arrangements and the development of the required plans and procedures to support them.

The implementation stage consists of the following processes:

- organisation and implementation planning
- implement stand-by arrangements
- implement risk reduction measures
- develop business recovery plans
- develop procedures
- carry out initial tests.

5.1 Establish organisation and develop implementation plans

Implementation of the business continuity strategy will highlight many issues relating to future operation of the proposed stand-by arrangements, business recovery plans and procedures. Awareness of these issues is essential for those individuals who are co-ordinating and controlling the recovery effort in the aftermath of a disaster or other incident.

To ensure that the resulting stand-by arrangements, plans and procedures are effective, implementation of the business continuity strategy must be led by those who will ultimately have responsibility for invoking the stand-by arrangements and managing the recovery effort.

The first process in the implementation stage addresses the following parallel activities:

- establish the command, control and communications structure
- develop a framework for business recovery plans
- develop implementation plans.

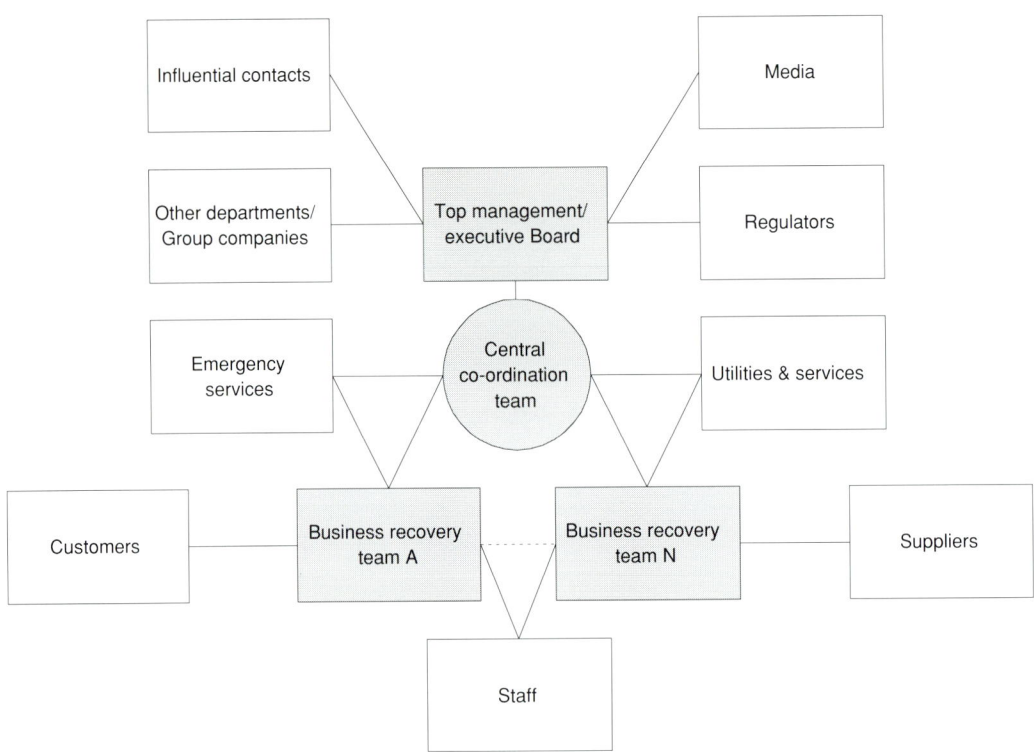

Figure 9 Typical command, control and communications structure

| Establish command, control and communications structure | A clear command, control and communications structure needs to be established to manage business recovery activities following a major business disruption. Recent case studies have highlighted problems that can occur when lines of communication break down or become confused. Lines of communication between various business recovery teams and the top executive or management Board and the means by which they will be established must be specified and agreed. |

Figure 9 illustrates how a command, control and communications structure might be established with the following components:

- top management/executive Board
- central co-ordination team
- business recovery teams.

Chapter 5
Stage 3 of the lifecycle – Implementation

Top management/executive Board

The top management/executive Board should retain overall authority and control within the organisation and is, typically, responsible for:

- crisis management
- public relations
- liaison with other departments/group organisations or companies, the media, regulators, influential contacts etc
- executive decisions.

Central co-ordination team

The central co-ordination team usually comprises people at one level below the top management/executive Board. These people have a good overall understanding of the business processes and business priorities, and have operational control over the groups that will invoke stand-by arrangements and recover the business.

The central co-ordination team, typically, contains individuals fulfilling some or all of the following co-ordination roles:

- management of the central co-ordination team, ie an overall Recovery Manager, (who might delegate responsibility for the day-to-day operational management levels to a specialist Business Continuity Manager)
- co-ordinators representing each critical business process or function, eg customer services, sales, production, distribution
- co-ordinators representing key support functions, such as accommodation and office services, security, computer systems and networking, telecommunications, personnel, finance and administration
- co-ordinators for critical additional activities that would need to be undertaken following a disaster or other incident, for example, salvage co-ordinator, public relations co-ordinator.

Figure 10 describes typical responsibilities for each member of the central co-ordination team. It is important to note that the ideal membership of the central co-ordination team and the allocation of responsibilities will vary from one organisation to the

Role	Typical responsibilities
Overall recovery manager	Overall co-ordination of the recovery operation
	Delegation of tasks to other members of the central co-ordination team
	Reporting to the top management/executive board
	Chairing meetings of the central co-ordination team
	Resolving conflicts
Co-ordinators representing operational business processes or functions	Co-ordinating the recovery of the process or function
	Liaison with the recovery manager and other members of the central co-ordination team
	Introduction of emergency working procedures
Accommodation and office services co-ordinator	Equipping accommodation and relocating staff
Security co-ordinator	Maintaining security at all sites, both original and stand-by premises
Computer systems and networks co-ordinator	Recovery of computer systems and networks
	Restoration of applications and data
Telecommunications co-ordinator	Recovery of telecommunications services
Personnel co-ordinator	Staff welfare, including establishment of any new working conditions, counselling, special transport needs
Finance and administration co-ordinator	Sanctioning emergency expenditure
	Payment of salaries and key invoices
	Introduction of emergency financial authorisation and control procedures
	Maintenance of an audit trail
Salvage co-ordinator	Recovery and restoration of damaged facilities and assets
Public relations co-ordinator	Ensuring that a positive and consistent message is presented to the news media.

Figure 10 Typical responsibilities for members of the central co-ordination team

next depending on the adopted business continuity strategy and the structure of the organisation. In some cases, roles may be combined, in others they may be shared. For example, where management of computer systems is delegated to business functions, responsibility for recovery of systems may need to be taken on by co-ordinators for the business functions, rather than by a central computer systems co-ordinator.

Collectively, the central co-ordination team, however, needs to cover all of the business functions and processes addressed by the strategy and all of the key support functions.

Following a disaster or incident, the central co-ordination team will usually be established at a suitably equipped emergency control centre (ECC).

Business recovery teams
The final part of the recovery organisation is usually a series of business recovery teams that support the central co-ordination team. The business recovery teams are responsible for actioning the business recovery plans for their own areas and for day to day liaison with staff, customers and suppliers. Each co-ordinator on the central co-ordination team may be supported by a business recovery team and hence separate teams may be required for each key support function, each critical business process or function and, possibly, for additional activities such as salvage and public relations.

Levels of authority
The business continuity initiative results in an agreed recovery strategy and business recovery plans to guide the organisation through all of the necessary actions to invoke stand-by arrangements and recover business processes. However, the recovery effort would be disrupted if:

- senior managers took decisions and issued instructions which conflicted with the strategy and plans
- multiple changes to decisions were made
- external bodies including the media were given the impression that the organisation was in a state of confusion, panic or chaos.

Well-defined levels of authority are essential to ensure that these problems do not arise. A typical allocation of authority is as follows:

- the top management/executive Board retains overall responsibility and authority for running the business and heads of individual business functions retain overall responsibility and authority for their functions

- all key decisions relating to the recovery, eg the decision to invoke the stand-by arrangements, are made by the Recovery Manager in consultation with the rest of the central co-ordination team. Certain decisions (identified in the business recovery plans) require confirmation from the Board. Where the Board are unavailable the Recovery Manager has the authority to action the decision

- requests for variations to the agreed business continuity strategy or plans which impact on other functions are raised by the appropriate co-ordinator, considered by the central co-ordination team and, if considered to be unacceptable, are rejected by the Recovery Manager. In making the decision, the Recovery Manager considers the views of other members of the central co-ordination team. For example, a request to upgrade a process to a higher priority can be vetoed by the accommodation co-ordinator if accommodation will not be available in time, by the computer systems co-ordinator if systems will not be available in time, and so on. Ultimately, the Board have to resolve any disputes that arise

- certain decisions (identified in the business recovery plans) will be considered to be firm once made and communicated, for example, the revised time by which products should be collected by distributors. These decisions should not be made too early but, bearing in mind recovery objectives, when a reasonable level of confidence exists that they can be achieved. Members of the central co-ordination team have the right to veto subsequent changes to these decisions if they will have an adverse impact on the overall recovery effort. Disputes

Chapter 5
Stage 3 of the lifecycle – Implementation

	are considered by the central co-ordination team and the Recovery Manager arbitrates. If necessary, the Board will be asked to resolve conflicts.
Develop a framework for business recovery plans	A business recovery plan (or more often an integrated set of plans) describes the actions to be taken from the moment that a disruption occurs. The plan(s) typically cover(s) activities such as emergency response, crisis management, damage assessment, salvage, deciding on whether or not to invoke stand-by arrangements, invocation of stand-by arrangements, recovery of business processes and, eventually, return-to-normal.

The business recovery plans, typically, contain a description of roles and responsibilities, action lists and reference data, often structured into discrete phases.

Figure 11 illustrates the recovery activities that typically need to be carried out, starting with emergency response and running through to eventual return to normal. These activities are shown grouped into three broad phases:

- an Alert phase during which an incident is reported, an initial damage assessment is completed and a decision is taken on whether to move to the Invocation and Recovery phase

- an Invocation and recovery phase during which stand-by arrangements are invoked and business processes are recovered

- a Return to normal phase during which the return to normal is planned, facilities and assets are refurbished, repaired or replaced, and operations are transferred from the stand-by arrangements to permanent arrangements.

The first two phases usually have to be carried out within strict time constraints and hence require the most detailed planning. Emergency response, salvage and crisis management activities may span several phases as illustrated in Figure 11.

Given that the recovery plans need to address all components of critical business processes, including staff, accommodation, computer systems and networks, data, telecommunications, paper records and so on, it is important to develop and agree a framework of business recovery plans before moving on to produce the detailed plans.

IT Infrastructure Library
A Guide to Business Continuity Management

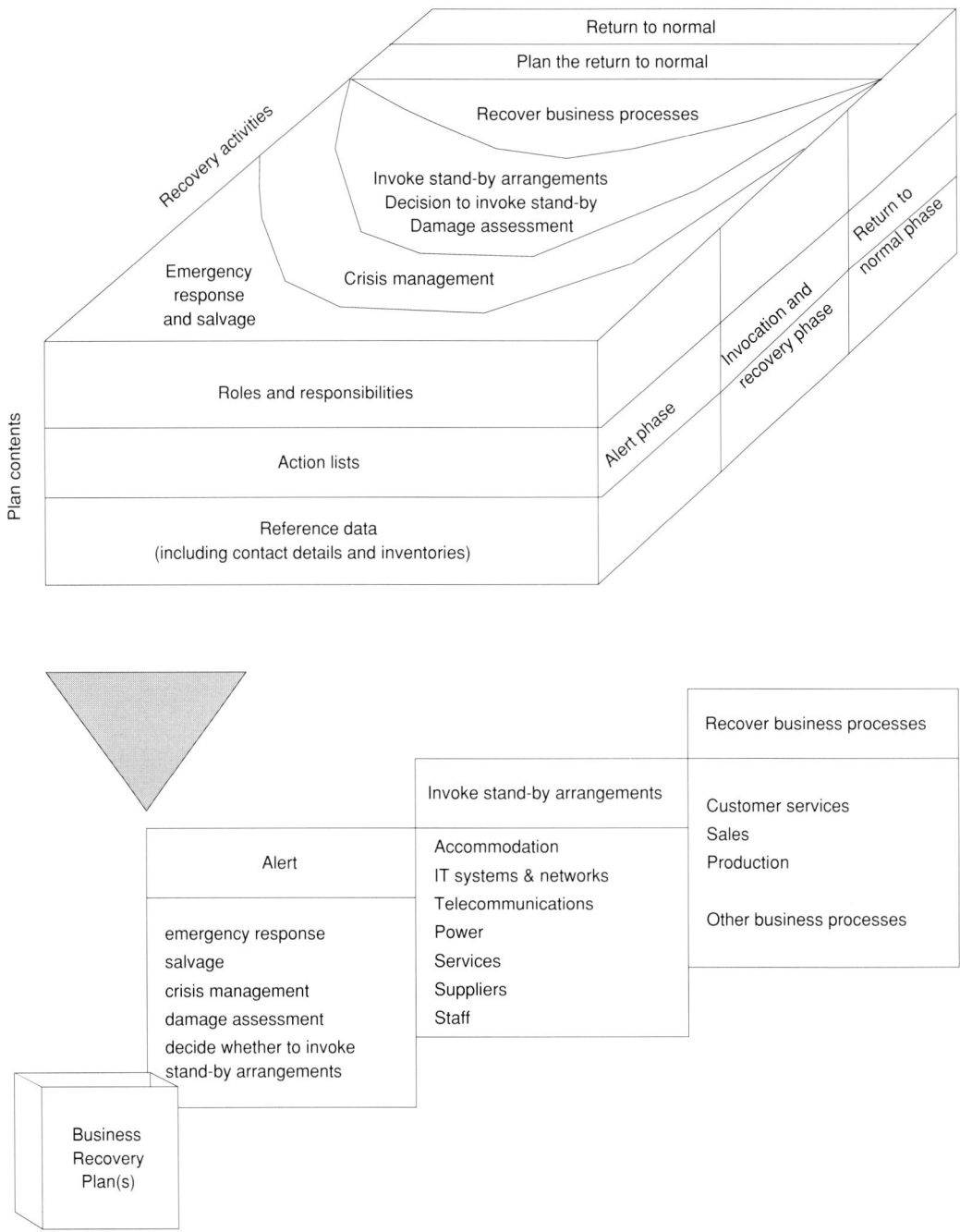

Figure 11 Typical structure and content of business recovery plans

Chapter 5
Stage 3 of the lifecycle – Implementation

The framework describes the complete set of plans to be produced and how they are to be structured. Figure 12 illustrates a typical set of integrated recovery plans, with:

- a master plan to co-ordinate the overall recovery effort
- a series of other plans for activities that may need to be co-ordinated across the organisation, eg crisis management and public relations, salvage and recovery of vital records
- plans for each key support function
- plans for each critical business process.

However, the number of plans to be produced, their scope and how they interrelate depends on the adopted command, control and communications structure and the agreed recovery strategy. Typically, a separate plan is produced for each business recovery team with overall co-ordination being provided by a master plan.

A framework of plans needs to be set which best meets the requirements of the organisation. This framework may include a large number of individual plans as shown on Figure 12 or a smaller number of plans each addressing several elements.

Example
Organisation X consists of largely autonomous business units each with responsibility for management of their own local computer systems. Responsibility for accommodation, office services, security and telecommunications remains with a central office services function and responsibility for personnel remains with a central human resources function.

Individual co-ordinators were appointed to the central co-ordination team from each autonomous business unit and from office services and human resources.

Individual plans were produced for each business unit covering: damage assessment; recovery of vital records, computer systems and networks; and resumption of business processes. A separate office services plan was produced covering damage assessment, salvage, security and recovery of accommodation, office equipment and telecommunications. A separate personnel plan covered personnel issues. Overall co-ordination was provided

IT Infrastructure Library
A Guide to Business Continuity Management

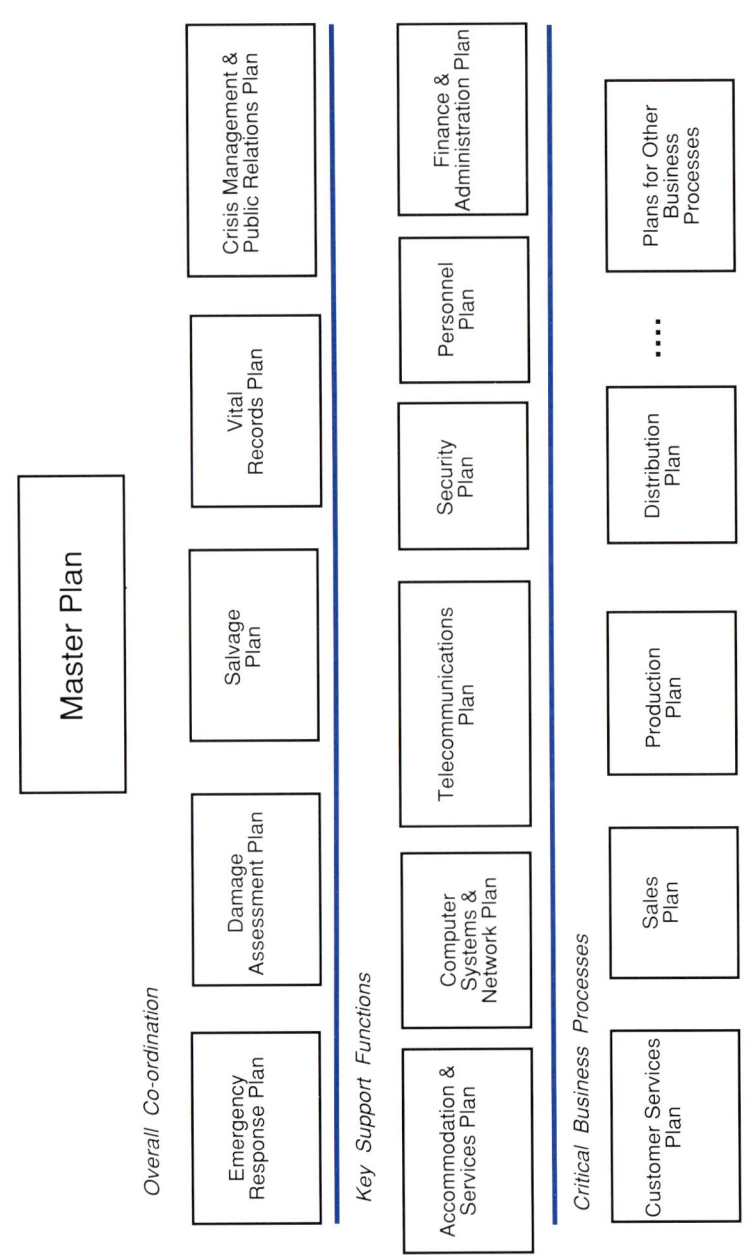

Figure 12 Typical 'logical' set of integrated business recovery plans

Chapter 5
Stage 3 of the lifecycle – Implementation

via a master plan which also addressed emergency response, crisis management and public relations.

The framework of business recovery plans allows an integrated set of plans to be produced to a common standard. Construction of the framework needs to take account of the agreed command, control and communications structure and also requirements for future maintenance of the plans.

Ideally, the framework will include plan templates which can be reviewed and agreed prior to completion of the individual plans. A sample template for a business recovery plan is included at Annex C. Section 5.4 describes the typical content of business recovery plans.

Develop implementation plans

Implementation of a business continuity strategy can be a major project in its own right which needs to be planned and managed. The final activity in the organisation and implementation planning process involves the development of implementation plans. These plans cover all of the activities that need to be undertaken during the implementation stage including:

- implementation of stand-by and risk reduction arrangements
- development of the business recovery plans and supporting procedures
- initial testing of the business recovery plans.

Since the business recovery plans and procedures say how and when the stand-by arrangements should be invoked, and since implementation of stand-by arrangements may be influenced by the tasks specified in the business recovery plans, the two processes of implementing stand-by arrangements and developing business recovery plans must be closely co-ordinated.

Use of the PRINCE project management method is recommended for the development of implementation plans.

5.2 Implement stand-by arrangements

The business continuity strategy is likely to be based around a series of stand-by arrangements for key components of the business process, eg accommodation, systems, telecommunications. Certain actions are likely to be necessary to implement (put into place) the selected stand-by arrangements, for example:

- preparing and equipping the emergency control centre and stand-by accommodation with furniture and power, telecommunications, and data cabling infrastructures

- purchasing and installing stand-by computer systems and network access points

- relocating computer systems or reconfiguring computer and voice communications networks

- making amendments to software to enable processing to be taken over by stand-by computer systems

- enhancing the policy and procedures for taking back-up copies of data

- installing stand-by telephone switchboards

- providing back-up power sources (eg generator cover) for critical areas

- negotiating with external service providers on their BCM arrangements and auditing them if possible

- selecting suppliers of commercial recovery services and negotiating contracts.

Training and new procedures may be required to operate, test and maintain the stand-by arrangements and to ensure that they are ready to be called into action when required.

Implementation of stand-by arrangements may need to address the following activities:

- refine requirements
- identify and select suppliers
- integrate solutions.

Refine requirements

The business continuity strategy will have determined how accommodation, systems, networks, paper records etc are to be recovered and business resumed. This is likely to have been at a fairly high level, sufficient, for example, to allow preparation of a business case. In some cases it may be necessary to commence implementation activities by refining the requirements specified in the business continuity strategy.

Chapter 5
Stage 3 of the lifecycle – Implementation

Example
The agreed strategy may have stated that:

- core teams of staff will be relocated to stand-by sites A and B
- twenty-five per cent of the PCs will be recovered within twenty-four hours via a call off contract, the rest from rush orders placed immediately post disaster, etc.

The actual allocation of business functions to stand-by sites A and B, the members of core teams and the precise identification of PC requirements for the call-off contract may not have been identified during the strategy definition. These and other detailed recovery arrangements need to be finalised before the stand-by arrangements can be implemented.

Identify and select suppliers	Where the strategy involves the use of commercial recovery services, for example, for stand-by accommodation or computer systems, a specification needs to be produced, against which interested vendors can provide quotations. The following factors should be considered when specifying commercial recovery services:

- facilities and services required
- the time within which these are needed following a disaster or other incident
- the degree to which access to the facilities or services will be required for testing
- the level of support required from the service provider's staff, both for maintenance of the arrangements and during invocation.

In evaluating commercial recovery services consideration should be given to the following:

- the ability of the vendor to meet the requirements specified
- the costs, including initial set-up costs, annual charges, invocation charges and costs for training and maintenance
- if the service is to be provided on the vendor's site, its location and the availability of communications services and transport

- if a mobile service is to be provided, access and siting arrangements

- the risk that the vendor will be unable to deliver the services contracted for.

This last factor is very important and is related to:

- the commercial viability of the vendor

- the ratio of total facilities/services available to those that have been contracted for

- any exclusion zones implemented.

Example
If a vendor has access to 500 PCs within twenty-four hours, but its total committed business (across all of its contracts) is to provide 12,000 PCs within twenty-four hours, the ratio would be 1:24.

Clearly, the higher the ratio the greater the risk that the vendor will be over-committed and unable to deliver when required. However, this worst case scenario needs to be considered in the light of the vendor's policy on accepting business from clients operating in the same neighbourhood who may be affected by the same incident.

Integrate solutions

It is likely that different teams will be implementing the stand-by options for accommodation, computer systems and networks, telecommunications and so on. However, these all need to work seamlessly during invocation and, hence, considerable care is required to ensure that integrated solutions are implemented. The approach recommended in section 5.1 of

- establishing the command, control and communications structure at an early stage during implementation, and

- allocating responsibility for implementation of stand-by arrangements to those who are responsible for invoking the arrangements

will help to ensure that this happens in practice.

5.3 Implement risk reduction measures

In addition to stand-by arrangements, the need for additional risk reduction measures may have been identified during the requirements and strategy stage. Any such risk reduction measures need to be implemented subject, of course, to value for money considerations. The activities involved in implementing the risk reduction measures are common to any procurement and/or implementation exercise. Other CCTA guidance (such as the Management of Risk Library, PRINCE and CRAMM) covers these activities in some detail.

Some risk reduction measures will themselves be procedures. As with stand-by arrangements, training and new procedures may also be required to operate, test and maintain the physical risk reduction measures.

5.4 Develop business recovery plan(s)

Business recovery plans are produced by completing the plan templates included as part of the business recovery plan framework. A sample business recovery plan template is included at Annex C. This shows that a typical plan consists of:

- an introductory section describing the purpose and scope of the plan, the various recovery phases, how the plan is structured, its relationship with other plans and an outline of how the overall recovery effort is to be organised and controlled
- a description of the team structure that will use the particular plan
- a set of task lists for the team or for individual roles within a team
- reference information that team members need to use in order to be able to carry out their allocated tasks, eg important contact details, asset inventories, access arrangements for stand-by sites.

The content of the introductory section will have been established already during definition of the business recovery plan framework and hence this part of the plan should be straightforward to produce. The remaining activities involved in this process are as follows:

- confirm the team structures that will use each plan and allocate staff to roles within the teams
- identify the tasks and collect the supporting reference information that needs to be incorporated into the plans
- produce the plans.

IT Infrastructure Library
A Guide to Business Continuity Management

Confirm the team structures	The overall co-ordinating business recovery plan (the master plan) guides the activities of the central co-ordination team. Hence the team structure for the master plan will already have been defined during the organisation and implementation planning process. Team structures are also required for each of the other plans included in the framework. Each team structure typically includes the following roles:

- a team leader, who is usually a member of the central co-ordination team

- co-ordinators for each key function or activity area covered by the plan

- team members to support each co-ordinator.

When deciding on the structure and composition of teams it is likely that teams from key support functions, for instance those dealing with recovery of accommodation, computer systems and networks, telecommunications etc will all be required to assist, probably with additional support from third party contractors. For finance, administration and critical business processes, it is likely that core teams of essential staff will be established initially to be followed by remaining staff when suitable facilities and services have been recovered.

Every key role within the team (team leader, team co-ordinators and key team members) needs to be defined and allocated to a staff member. It is possible that in a major disaster staff may have been killed or injured and therefore at least one, and preferably two, deputies should be assigned to each of these key roles.

Figure 13 illustrates a sample team structure for a computer systems and networks business recovery plan. It should be noted that this is only an example and, in fact, the team structures put in place would usually reflect the existing organisational structure within the department or group.

Identify tasks and collect reference information	When the appropriate team structures are in place, attention can turn to:

- identifying the tasks that the team needs to carry out in the event of a disaster or other incident

- collecting the reference information that will support the execution of these tasks.

Chapter 5
Stage 3 of the lifecycle – Implementation

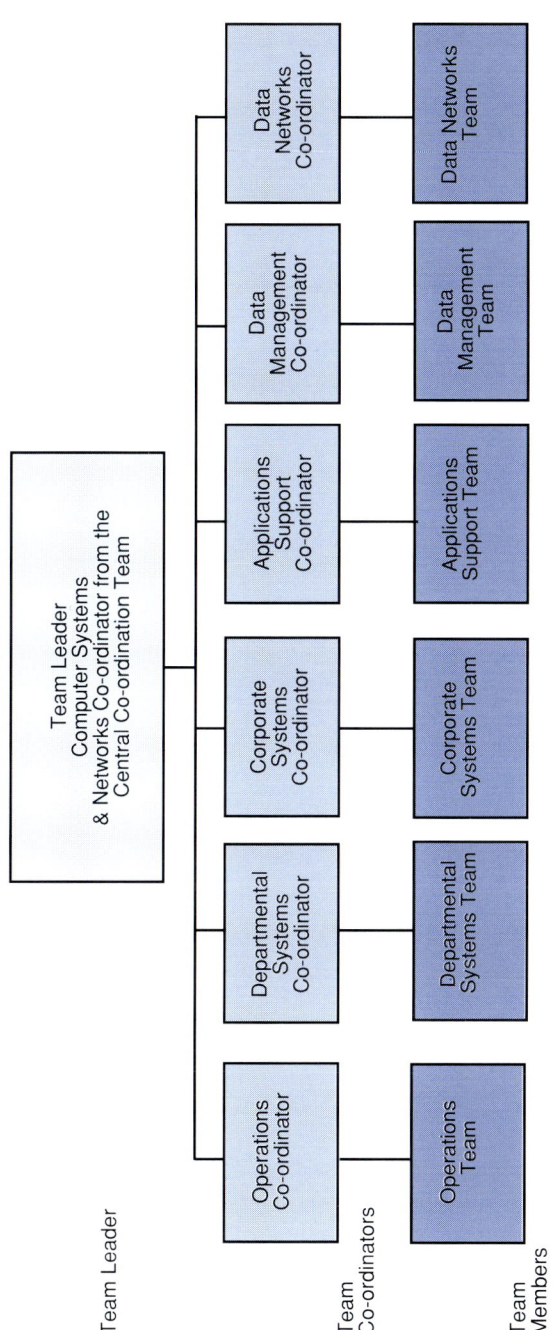

Figure 13 Sample team structure for a computer systems and networks business recovery plan

It is highly recommended that tasks are identified and reference information is collected by those individuals who will be carrying out the tasks in the event of an incident. Without this, there is a serious risk that incomplete or inadequate tasks will be specified. Conversely, involvement in the process will generate confidence in the BCM initiative and assist with education and awareness.

The task lists should not be over complicated or too detailed but should clearly specify the actions that are required; in particular those that require communications with other teams or third parties. A good rule of thumb is that the task lists must contain the minimum information necessary to enable the tasks to be understood and actioned by deputies. Reference data should be only that which is essential to support the recovery effort – reference data that could be obtained from other sources or re-created easily can be omitted from the plans.

Figure 12 describes a typical 'logical' set of business recovery plans as including:

- overall co-ordinating plans including a master plan and plans addressing emergency response, crisis management and public relations, damage assessment, salvage and vital records
- plans for key support functions such as accommodation and services, computer systems and networks, telecommunications, security, personnel, and finance and administration
- plans for critical business processes or functions.

The contents of these plans are discussed below.

Master plan
The master plan guides the actions of the central co-ordinating team through:

- notification of an incident
- receipt of initial damage assessments
- initiation of activities such as crisis management and salvage

- the decision on whether or not to invoke stand-by arrangements
- initiation of communications channels with staff, suppliers and third parties
- initiation of the invocation phase, if stand-by arrangements are to be invoked
- the recovery phase.

In addition to these, the master plan guides the overall co-ordination of the Invocation and recovery phase and, eventually the Return to normal phase. This sequence of events is ordered through regular meetings of the central co-ordination team during which:

- progress is monitored
- decisions are taken
- actions are allocated to members of the central co-ordination team.

The Recovery Manager as leader of the central co-ordination team will liaise closely with the top management/executive Board.

Emergency response

The way in which an organisation responds in the immediate aftermath of a disaster has a direct influence on the safety of its staff, the protection of its assets and the ease with which the business can be recovered. A successful emergency response requires suitable procedures to have been produced, distributed to staff and tested prior to the incident.

Emergency response procedures should therefore be produced and issued to staff covering:

- the alarm signals and their meaning
- evacuation procedures
- assembly points following evacuation from the building
- what to do if suspicious items are spotted, or if a fire or other incidents are discovered
- immediate actions that can be taken to protect staff and assets, eg use of fire extinguishing systems
- key lines of communication to initiate business recovery activities

- guidance on the immediate actions to be taken by those staff who are members of the central co-ordination team or business recovery teams, eg report to an Emergency Control Centre
- guidance on actions to be taken by staff who hear about the incident at home via the news media, eg contact an alternative office for instructions, listen to local radio announcements, call an information line, wait at home until they are contacted etc.

Procedures are also required for those involved in dealing with the emergency services and notifying next of kin.

Damage assessment
Invocation of stand-by arrangements unnecessarily could have a major disruptive effect on the organisation and should only be undertaken when the situation warrants it. Conversely, unnecessary delay in ordering invocation could result in an escalation of potential business impacts.

In some situations, such as a localised fire or technical failure the extent of the damage or impact on the business processes may not be immediately apparent and an urgent damage assessment would be required. For major incidents such as a terrorist bomb or large fire, the need to invoke would be quite clear. However, a damage assessment would still be required to determine the extent of damage to the organisation's assets and to assess the extent to which recovery or salvage of assets was possible.

The damage assessment plan typically assesses damage to :

- the building structure
- building services such as water supply, power supply, fire alarms, lighting, PA systems, plumbing and public health
- computer systems and networks
- telecommunication services and equipment
- office equipment and other assets
- vital records.

Pre-prepared damage assessment forms should be used to ensure that all relevant information is collected and referenced correctly.

It should be remembered that access to the site will be restricted by the emergency services in the immediate aftermath of an incident. For example, a 500 metre security cordon may be placed around a building for 24 hours following a terrorist blast. For any significant incident, the approval of the emergency services is required before the building can be re-occupied. The Health and Safety Executive or the Factory Inspectorate can also restrict access as, in certain circumstances, may insurance companies.

Salvage
It is very unlikely that any incident would cause irreparable damage to all assets. In many cases salvage would be possible. While access can be hindered by access restrictions as described above, speed is of the essence to prevent further deterioration. Salvage usually requires specialist expertise and covers such actions as:

- decontamination, covering dangerous substances such as asbestos and chemicals as well as smoke and dirty water
- removal of dust, debris and glass fragments
- stabilisation of the environment, including ventilation and de-humidification
- recovery of data from damaged electronic media
- recovery of damaged paper records.

Insurance companies will appoint a loss adjuster to assist with preparation of a claim. Valuable time can be saved if the loss adjuster is identified and the plan to use specialist salvage experts is agreed prior to an incident occurring.

It should be remembered that unless assets are insured under a replacement as new policy the full replacement cost of assets are not covered.

The salvage plan needs to be closely related to the damage assessment plan. The salvage plan defines the actions necessary to initiate and control the salvage operation, and contains contact details for specialist salvage firms. Stand-by assets for critical business processes will, depending on the agreed strategy, have already been established or will be acquired immediately post-disaster. However, the strategy for recovery of less critical processes may rely, in part, on the use of salvaged assets. Where this is the case, decision criteria should be established to cover the situation where salvage is not possible or is delayed.

Vital records

Vital records cover both data held on electronic media and records held on paper or fiche. Loss of data on electronic media can be protected against by suitable back-up and restoration procedures which would usually be addressed by the computer systems and network recovery plan. Large volumes of paper or fiche records are much more difficult to protect in this way but they may:

- contain essential historical information
- be contracts or other legal documents (perhaps original signed documents)
- contain other information that is critical to the business process.

When data protection law is extended to manual records, organisations will have a legal responsibility to take appropriate measures to protect the records. For some businesses, there may also be legal implications concerning the availability of original source documents, minimum retention periods and copyright issues associated with the duplication of certain documents.

Recovery of paper/fiche records may be addressed by plans for individual business processes or functions or, alternatively, be co-ordinated via an overall vital records plan. The vital records plan will typically cover:

- procedures for retrieving original, alternative or duplicated records
- procedures for salvage of damaged records (although these may be contained in a separate salvage plan).

Effective implementation of these recovery procedures will only be possible if suitable document management procedures are in place prior to the event, eg correct referencing of vital records, use of appropriate storage containers and marking of cabinets and safes containing critical documents.

Crisis management and public relations
Crisis management and public relations are very closely interlinked and are the responsibility of the top management/executive Board. In many organisations, particularly those in sectors such as financial services, the value and profitability of the business is heavily reliant on the confidence that customers, shareholders and the market in general have in the organisation and its top management team. A situation in which the organisation is perceived to be in chaos must be avoided.

While no one can be expected to provide 100 per cent protection against a disaster or other incident occurring, top management will be expected to have put in place suitable plans to mitigate the impact and to provide continuity of the business. Equally important, the organisation needs to be seen to have put such plans in place.

The crisis management and public relations plan should address the criteria against which certain key actions will be authorised, for example, the trigger points at which:

- trading in a financial market is to be temporarily suspended
- products suspected of contamination are to be temporarily withdrawn from sale
- services are to be temporarily withdrawn.

In all cases the responsibilities for public relations must be carefully defined and key messages to be put across to customers, shareholders, suppliers and the media must have been identified and rehearsed in advance. The services of public relations companies specialising in crisis management may prove useful to some organisations. Where part of the business has been affected, the crisis management plan should seek, as far as possible, to isolate the affected processes and reduce the risk to other parts of the business.

While it will be the views of top management that will be sought by third parties, care must be taken to ensure that the views given are not compromised or contradicted by other statements from elsewhere in the organisation. All staff should therefore be made aware of the procedures for communicating with third parties in the event of a disaster. Attention should also be given to:

- publishing the telephone number of an enquiry service for the media
- creating a list of possible questions that may be raised with agreed answers
- preparing template press statements that could be completed and issued quickly
- instructing switchboard operators on how to handle enquiries.

All press statements and other relevant information should also be circulated to staff.

Plans for key support functions and critical business processes

The task lists and reference information for key support functions and critical business processes must be specific to particular aspects of the recovery operation, eg recover computer systems, resume the customer services process. Figure 14 describes typical activities and typical reference information for each plan.

Chapter 5
Stage 3 of the lifecycle – Implementation

Plan type	Typical alert phase tasks	Typical invocation and recovery phase tasks	Typical reference information
Accommodation and services	Assess damage to the site and services	Invoke any recovery contracts for accommodation and building services	Contact details for staff, suppliers, contractors, lease holders, emergency services
	Advise on whether stand-by accommodation arrangements should be invoked	Place orders with contractors for building work, electrical work etc	Maps and floor plans for stand-by sites
	Liaise with emergency services	Place orders for replacement assets	Asset registers for equipment
	Advise on the likely time within which the building can be reoccupied	Prepare stand-by accommodation for occupancy	
	Put contractors and providers of recovery services on stand-by	Redirect post and arrange distribution of incoming post	
Computer systems and networks	Assess damage to computer systems and networks	Invoke recovery contracts for computer systems and networks	Contact details for staff, suppliers, contractors
	Put contractors and providers of recovery services on stand-by	Place orders with contractors for cabling, installation etc	Maps and floor plans for stand-by sites
	Advise on the likely time within which computer systems or networks could be recovered	Place orders for replacement equipment and supplies	Cabling diagrams Asset register for computer equipment and networks
	Advise on whether stand-by computer systems and network arrangements should be invoked	Arrange installation of replacement equipment	'Pro-forma' emergency support and administration procedures
		Restore software and data on stand-by equipment	
		Establish data networks	
		Test systems and networks and hand over to users	
		Implement emergency support and administration procedures, eg help desk, back-up arrangements	

Figure 14 Typical contents of business recovery plans for key support services and critical business processes

Plan type	Typical alert phase tasks	Typical invocation and recovery phase tasks	Typical reference information
Telecomms	Assess damage to telecommunications equipment and services	Invoke any recovery contracts for telecommunications services	Contact details for staff, suppliers, contractors, telecomms service providers
	Put contractors and providers of recovery services on stand-by	Provide mobile telephones	Maps and floor plans for stand-by sites
	Advise on the likely time within which telecomms services could be recovered	Place orders with contractors for cabling, installation etc	Asset register of telecomms equipment
	Advise on whether stand-by telecomms arrangements should be invoked	Place orders for replacement equipment and supplies	'Pro-forma' emergency internal telephone directory
		Arrange for lines to be delivered to stand-by sites	
		Arrange for messages to be broadcast to callers until the service is recovered	
		Issue an emergency internal telephone directory	
		Arrange for additional switchboard operators as required	
Security	Liaise with the police regarding the control of access to damaged buildings	Monitor and control the removal of assets from damaged buildings	Contact details for staff police, security contractors etc
	Provide security for damaged buildings	Provide security for stand-by sites	Map and floor plans for stand-by sites
	Remove or secure valuable items such as cash, negotiable instruments, confidential material	Issue emergency security procedures to staff at stand-by sites, eg staff passes	'Pro-forma' emergency security procedures

Figure 14 (*continued*) Typical contents of business recovery plans for key support services and critical business processes

Chapter 5
Stage 3 of the lifecycle – Implementation

Plan type	Typical alert phase tasks	Typical invocation and recovery phase tasks	Typical reference information
Personnel	Assess any injuries to staff	Keep staff informed of the situation	Contact details for staff, counselling services, staff agencies etc
		Reassure staff that their jobs are secure, they will be paid on time, authorised additional expenses will be paid	Allocation of staff to core teams
		Provide staff with access to a counselling service if required	
		Co-ordinate transport arrangements to stand-by sites	
		Organise additional temporary staff if required	
Finance and administration	Assess the status of valuable items such as cash, negotiable instruments, cheque signing machines etc	Liaise with security co-ordinator over security for valuable items	Contact details for staff, suppliers, bankers etc
			Allocation of staff to core teams
		If necessary arrange for alternative or extended banking facilities, eg cash, cheques to be paid into an alternative branch	Financial records
		Order replacement cheques, cash books, cash, cheque signing machines etc	'Pro-forma' emergency procedures
		Prioritise payments	Stocks of emergency forms, eg for advances on expenses
		Liaise with personnel co-ordinator over salary payments	
		Authorise payments on account to key suppliers if appropriate	
		Introduce emergency financial controls	

Figure 14 (*continued*) Typical contents of business recovery plans for key support services and critical business processes

IT Infrastructure Library
A Guide to Business Continuity Management

Plan type	Typical alert phase tasks	Typical invocation and recovery phase tasks	Typical reference information
Critical business process	Assess the impact and manage changes to critical assets and services	Brief staff, customers, key suppliers as appropriate	Contact details for staff, customers, suppliers etc
		Liaise with accommodation, computer systems and telecomms co-ordinators over likely timescales for recovery	Allocation of staff to core teams

Inventory of assets |
		Order replacement assets or services	'Pro-forma' briefing notes for customers and suppliers
		Retrieve vital records	
		Introduce emergency procedures	

Figure 14 (*continued*) Typical contents of business recovery plans for key support services and critical business processes

Important note about Figure 14

It should be noted that the content of business recovery plans will vary greatly depending on the recovery objectives, the recovery strategy and the nature of the organisation. When reviewing Figure 14 the reader should bear in mind that:

- this is not an exhaustive list
- tasks are described only at a high level
- tasks are not necessarily shown in an order of sequence or priority
- the actual allocation of tasks to plans will depend on the business recovery plan framework and may not be as shown here.

Chapter 5
Stage 3 of the lifecycle – Implementation

Produce the plans	Once the tasks associated with each plan in the framework have been identified, and the necessary reference information has been collected, the plans can be constructed in accordance with the framework.

There are two common approaches to structuring task lists and reference data:

- the task lists can refer to reference data held elsewhere in the document, perhaps in appendices
- the task lists and reference data can be integrated so that each task will be followed by the reference data required to carry out the task.

Software packages, if they are used to help develop business resumption plans, tend to support one or other of these approaches and sometimes both. In deciding on the approach to be taken, account should be taken of:

- the ease of use in a disaster situation
- the ease with which the plans could be maintained.

Where reference information such as contact details and asset registers is available elsewhere within the organisation, careful consideration should be given to whether this should be duplicated in the plan or referenced by the plan. Generally, where information is already held for other business reasons, it may be more cost effective to protect and back-up this information to guarantee its availability in an emergency rather than duplicate it within the business recovery plan.

Issue the plans for testing	On completion of this activity the business recovery plans are ready for issue to team members for initial testing.
5.5 Develop procedures	Task lists within business recovery plans must be distinguished from the detailed procedures which may be necessary to support particular tasks and also from the detailed procedures that a business function might follow to run its business in an emergency. Procedures tend to relate to complex activities or activities that must be undertaken differently, or which are only required, in an emergency situation. Inclusion of detailed procedures in the task lists themselves would lead to unwieldy documents and mask the purpose of the plans.

Examples of procedures include:

- manual procedures for the recording of orders, credit checking and issuing of invoices
- procedures for the emergency transfer of business from one external service provider to another
- procedures to install and test replacement hardware and networks and to restore software and data to a common baseline that is consistent across all business processes.

The need for procedures is identified during development of the business recovery plans. Procedures are fundamental to ensuring the effective recovery of the business in line with recovery objectives. Procedures are usually of a detailed nature and describe all the necessary steps in support of a particular recovery task.

Some procedures may already exist within the organisation, while others will need to be developed specifically for the purpose of business continuity management. Procedures will usually be developed to the organisation's own standards for presentation and layout.

Procedures can be either attached to the business recovery plans (perhaps as an appendix) or maintained as separate documents. If the latter approach is adopted, back-up copies of the procedures must be stored in a secure location with details of the location and access arrangements contained in the business recovery plans.

In addition to procedures supporting the business recovery tasks, procedures may also be required to support risk reduction measures. These could include:

- procedures for controlling access of staff and visitors
- procedures for monitoring CCTV surveillance and investigating suspicious incidents.

Risk reduction procedures need to be maintained as changes occur within the organisation and this is more likely to be achieved if they can be incorporated into broader security procedures.

Chapter 5
Stage 3 of the lifecycle – Implementation

5.6   Carry out initial tests

Testing is a critical part of the overall BCM process and is the only way of ensuring that the selected strategy, stand-by arrangements, business recovery plans and procedures will work in practice. Initial testing is undertaken as part of the implementation stage to check that the strategy has been implemented effectively and to allow necessary revisions to be made before the plans are formally issued.

During this activity test objectives, test types and test scenarios are set. It should be noted, however, that even the most comprehensive test cannot cover everything. For example, it is not possible to test realistically the way in which staff will react in a crisis when colleagues may have been injured or killed. The business recovery plans need to make an allowance for this.

Tests on risk reduction measures should also be planned where appropriate. These may include:

- technical tests, to check that technical risk reduction measures are working correctly
- penetration tests, to check that the physical, technical, personnel and procedural risk reduction measures are able to prevent or at least detect attacks or other incidents.

The initial testing process consists of the following activities:

- develop test objectives
- decide test type(s)
- establish test scenario(s)
- develop test plans
- perform tests
- document and publish test results.

Develop test objectives

Typical objectives for an initial test are to:

- provide a practical evaluation of the risk reduction and business recovery strategies
- ensure that the tasks detailed in the business recovery plans and the procedures are consistent with the actual tasks and procedures necessary to achieve the recovery objectives
- highlight any requirements for changes to the strategy, plans and procedures

79

- ensure that the stand-by arrangements and plans will work when invoked.

Decide test type(s) — Business recovery tests can typically be categorised into four types:

Walkthroughs
A paper exercise in which a team (or teams) working to a set scenario utilises the business recovery plans in committee forum to 'walkthrough' a business recovery.

Technical component tests
Tests of specific technical components of the strategy and plans, for example:

- invocation of a commercial disaster recovery contract
- gaining emergency access to a stand-by site
- diverting telecommunications services to a stand-by site.

Technical component tests can usually be undertaken without significant involvement from users in business functions.

Business component tests
Tests in which the recovery of a business process or business function is tested. This must always involve the business functions concerned.

Full tests
Tests which replicate, as closely as possible, the invocation of all stand-by arrangements and the recovery of business processes.

Establish test scenario(s) — All tests are undertaken against defined test scenarios which are described as realistically as possible. Examples of test scenarios could include:

- a fire on floors 3 to 7 of building A has resulted in denial of access to the entire building for an unknown period, the incident happened during the night, there are no staff injuries
- a chemical spillage has occurred outside the building during the working day, an area of 1 mile radius has been evacuated for up to twenty-four hours, certain key (named) staff have been taken to hospital
- a major (named) supplier has been put into receivership

Chapter 5
Stage 3 of the lifecycle – Implementation

- a bomb has exploded at the local telephone exchange, all services through that exchange will be disrupted for up to ten days.

Develop test plans

A risk exists that certain types of test, if not properly planned, could themselves cause serious disruption to the organisation. Careful consideration should therefore be given to the nature and timing of tests. Issues to consider in preparing a test plan are:

- identification of the test team; during initial testing this should be the team that prepared the plan – later tests can involve deputies
- the time to be allocated to testing
- the level of resource to be dedicated to the test, including staff, accommodation and office equipment, computer systems and networks, telecommunications
- financial limits
- the permitted level of disruption to normal working.

The test plan does not need to be prescriptive in terms of the actions to be taken by the team(s) during the test since the objective of the exercise is to test how well the recovery procedures are documented and understood by the team members. However, careful planning is required to ensure that the actions used to simulate the disaster do not trigger off the very situation that the business recovery plans are designed to address.

Perform tests

Initial tests will be performed in line with the test plans and objectives. The tests need to be monitored and this is typically achieved through:

- each person involved in the test maintaining a test diary
- an umpire maintaining an umpire's log.

The test diary monitors events that happen and also when significant events are progressed, such as:

- the time that notification of the incident was received
- assumptions made in lieu of physical testing
- times that business recovery objectives were achieved

- any incidents that question the viability of the plans
- details and times of contacts with third parties
- details of any *live incidents* affecting the test
- the time the test was terminated.

The umpire's log is similar to the diaries except that the umpire is more concerned in assessing the different components of the test and how they interrelate.

Document and publish test results

Following each test, results are documented and published ready for necessary amendments to be made to the strategy, stand-by arrangements, risk reduction measures, business recovery plans and procedures.

6 Stage 4 of the lifecycle – Operational management

On completion of the implementation and planning stage, the BCM lifecycle moves into operational management of business continuity. This is a set of ongoing BCM processes rather than the project related work which characterised Stages 2 and 3.

The importance of effective operational management for business continuity cannot be overstated. In reaching this stage of the BCM lifecycle, most organisations will have made a significant investment in both staff time and financial resources. If the organisation for BCM has been established correctly and business recovery team members have been involved in implementation of the strategy and initial testing a high level of awareness and understanding about BCM should exist.

However, all organisations undergo continual change and the strategy and plans, and the individual understanding of team members, can rapidly become out of date unless suitable management structures and processes are in place.

Chapter 4 of the CCTA volume, *An Introduction to Business Continuity Management*, describes a recommended management structure for the operational management of BCM.

A key component of the management structure for the operational management stage will be a Business Continuity Manager who will advise the Management Board on BCM policy and strategy and ensure that the strategy and plans remain up to date. The Business Continuity Manager will, typically, be (or report to) the Recovery Manager in charge of the central co-ordination team.

The following processes are included within the operational management stage:

- testing
- education and awareness
- training
- change management
- assurance.

6.1 Testing

Following on from initial testing, an ongoing programme of testing should be established covering a suitable mix of walkthroughs, technical component tests, business component tests and, if appropriate, full tests. Full tests, if they are undertaken at all, are likely to be relatively rare because of the level of disruption and business risk associated with them. The bulk of the test programme is therefore likely to consist of modular tests of technical and business components. Regular walkthroughs of recovery plans will serve a dual purpose of testing and maintaining awareness amongst team members.

The frequency of testing will depend upon the rate of change within the organisation, the adopted recovery strategy and the recovery objectives. Stand-by arrangements for the most critical business processes will need to be tested regularly, at least once a year, with less frequent testing of other components.

The test programme can become progressively more demanding over time, for example:

- starting with tests where staff are warned in advance and moving on to those which are initiated without warning
- starting with tests where all staff are allowed to take part and moving progressively on to those where only deputies are allowed to participate.

Careful planning will be required for all tests to ensure that they do not, themselves, result in a major disruption to the business. Tests must be carefully monitored to ensure that requirements for change are identified and acted upon.

Section 5.6 provides more detail on testing.

6.2 Education and awareness

Education and awareness of business continuity policy, strategies and plans will be essential for the ongoing success of the BCM initiative within the organisation. The aim must be to get to a situation where management consider the business continuity implications of all major business activities as part of their normal routine. Achieving this aim will depend upon the existence of effective policies and management structures for BCM. Chapter 6 of the CCTA volume, *An Introduction to Business Continuity Management*, describes how to generate awareness of and commitment to BCM.

Chapter 6
Stage 4 of the lifecycle – Operational management

As described above, testing is a good way of educating and raising awareness for key team members. For example:

- regular walkthroughs of business recovery plans will ensure that key staff remain aware of their responsibilities and the actions expected of them
- technical and functional tests will raise awareness and educate staff about potential problems and issues to be faced.

In addition to testing, an ongoing programme of education and awareness is likely to be required, with the objectives of ensuring that:

- staff understand the risks, remain vigilant and know how to respond in the event of a disaster or other serious incident
- changes or issues that could affect the business continuity strategy and plans are identified and acted upon
- team members, and deputies, remain fully aware of their responsibilities and the actions expected of them.

The following methods of delivery should be considered:

- regular briefings to all staff on the need for vigilance and on emergency procedures
- demonstration of stand-by facilities to key staff, eg inspection of the stand-by accommodation
- use of the organisation's newsletter to maintain the profile of BCM
- regular progress reports to the Board and a regular agenda item on other management committees.

Consideration should also be given to the most effective method of presentation. As an example:

- lengthy briefing notices or articles in a newsletter may be less effective than an interview or question and answer style presentation

- verbal briefings may be enhanced by video clips or an exhibition with photographs and demonstrations.

In-house public relations or media departments will usually be a good source of ideas on these issues.

In some organisations, education and awareness programmes may already exist for other related purposes (eg fire prevention, security) and it may prove beneficial to integrate BCM into these.

Wherever possible senior management should be involved in the education and awareness programme to demonstrate commitment from the top. The overall aim must be to get to a stage where management considers business continuity issues in relation to and prior to making key business decisions. This will allow a balanced assessment of the risks to inform the decision making process.

6.3 Training

In addition to education and awareness, certain staff may require specific training on particular elements of the recovery strategy. Examples include training on:

- alternative processes or systems that may be used in an emergency
- how to reconfigure computer systems or networks for use in an emergency
- manual systems that may be used whilst an automated system is being recovered.

Particular care should be taken with the training needs of deputies. When called into action during an emergency (due to unavailability of the first named team member) deputies will be required to carry out actions which may not be part of their normal routine. The training and testing programmes should therefore ensure that deputies have the required level of competence to execute the actions required of them.

6.4 Review and change control

The stand-by arrangements, risk reduction measures and business recovery plans put in place during the implementation stage will have reflected the requirements of the business at the time. A change management process covering review and change control is required to ensure that the strategy and plans remain up to date and effective.

Chapter 6
Stage 4 of the lifecycle – Operational management

Further guidance is provided in the CCTA IT Infrastructure Library guide on *Change Management*.

Changes can be considered under two categories:

Maintenance changes
Maintenance changes are those which are necessary to keep business continuity plans up to date but which will not affect the underlying recovery objectives or business continuity strategy. Examples include staff resigning or transferring to new positions, changed contact details for suppliers, minor changes to system configurations, and where an error is discovered in the plans but does not affect the underlying recovery objectives and strategy.

Review changes
Review changes are those that will, or may, affect the underlying recovery objectives and strategy. Examples include the introduction of new business processes, major changes to systems, acquisition or disposal of property, changed risks etc.

The change management process

The approach to managing change will vary depending on whether the change is classed as maintenance or review.

The change management process consists of the following activities:

- determine a change strategy
- identify the need for change
- action the changes
- revise plans and procedures.

Determine a change strategy

Well-defined ownership of the strategy and plans is a fundamental requirement for effective change management. A typical allocation of ownership will be as follows:

- the business continuity strategy and the master plan will be owned by the Recovery Manager (the person in charge of the central co-ordination team during response to an incident) or by a Business Continuity Manager acting on behalf of the Recovery Manager

(as mentioned in 5.1, since the Recovery Manager will be a senior person, responsibility for the day to day operational management activities is often delegated to a

IT Infrastructure Library
A Guide to Business Continuity Management

specialist Business Continuity Manager. The remainder of this chapter refers to the responsibilities of the Business Continuity Manager rather than the Recovery Manager)

- all other plans will be owned by the relevant team leader, eg the computer systems and networks plan by the computer systems and networks co-ordinator, the sales plan by the sales co-ordinator and so on.

This allocation will give responsibility for business recovery plans to those people who are most dependent on them and will support the following typical change management strategy.

Maintenance changes

Maintenance changes will be identified and undertaken by the appropriate plan owner. The plan owner will issue replacement pages, or if appropriate a replacement document, to plan holders in line with the distribution list for the plan. If the change will, or may, have implications for other plans the initiating plan owner will notify other relevant plan owner(s).

Review changes

Review changes will be identified by plan owners, or other members of the central co-ordination or business recovery teams, and notified to the Business Continuity Manager. The Business Continuity Manager will co-ordinate the activities to:

- review the change and assess the impact on recovery objectives, stand-by arrangements, risk reduction measures and business recovery plans
- implement the required changes.

Review changes should be addressed immediately if the Business Continuity Manager considers that they could seriously undermine the business continuity strategy. Otherwise, they will be incorporated into a regular review programme, and considered at the next scheduled review, typically every six months.

Identify the need for change

The change strategy will rely on the need for change being identified by plan owners or other individuals. Procedures will, therefore, need to be established within each business area to ensure that requirements for change are identified.

Chapter 6
Stage 4 of the lifecycle – Operational management

Change	Responsibility for identifying change	Responsibility for action
Business or operational change		
Introduction, disposal of, or change to a business function or process	Relevant process co-ordinators and team member(s) to notify business continuity manager	Business continuity manager to co-ordinate
Change of business strategy		
Reorganisation		
Merger, acquisition, divestment etc		
Change in the performance or perceived importance of particular business processes		
Changes to accommodation		
Property acquired or disposed of	Accommodation co-ordinator to notify business continuity manager	Business continuity manager to co-ordinate
Relocation of business functions		
Changes to computer systems or networks		
Computer systems/networks introduced, replaced or disposed of	Computer systems and networks co-ordinator or, if appropriate, other co-ordinators to notify business continuity manager	Business continuity manager to co-ordinate
Changes in technical platform used (including hardware, software, comms)		
Outsourcing of systems/networks		

Figure 15 Typical review changes

Change	Responsibility for identifying change	Responsibility for action
Changes to telecomms		
Telecomms services introduced, replaced or disposed of	Telecommunications co-ordinator to notify Business Continuity Manager	Business Continuity Manager to co-ordinate
Changes to technology used		
Changes affecting suppliers		
Reallocation of business to suppliers (including rationalisation down to a smaller number)	Relevant co-ordinators to notify Business Continuity Manager	Business Continuity Manager to co-ordinate
Introduction of new suppliers		
Changes in the perceived risks		
Increased or reduced threat of attack, disaster or other incident	Relevant co-ordinators to notify Business Continuity Manager	Business Continuity Manager to co-ordinate
Increase or reduction in the vulnerability to attack, disaster or other incident, eg the introduction of single points of failure		
Identification of new risk reduction measures or stand-by arrangements, eg new commercial recovery services		

Figure 15 (*continued*) Typical review changes

Note to Figure 15
Although the Business Continuity Manager will co-ordinate the actions necessary to handle the changes described above, contributions will be required from relevant recovery team members, eg changes relating to telecommunications will require significant input from the telecommunications co-ordinator.

Chapter 6
Stage 4 of the lifecycle – Operational management

Change	Responsibility for identifying change	Responsibility for action
Revision to task lists	Relevant plan owner	Plan owner
Change of team members	Relevant plan owner	Plan owner
Changes to home contact details for staff	Relevant plan owner	Plan owner
Changes to procedures	Relevant plan owner	Plan owner
Changes to details of other contacts, such as suppliers, contractors, key customers etc	Relevant plan owner	Plan owner
Changes to minimum facilities required by core teams	Relevant plan owner	Plan owner
Changes to the allocation of accommodation at stand-by sites	Accommodation co-ordinator	Accommodation co-ordinator
Changes to asset registers	Accommodation, computer systems and networks, telecomms and other relevant co-ordinators	Owners of asset registers
Changes to forms	Relevant plan owner	Plan owner
Changes to checklists	Relevant plan owner	Plan owner
Changes to register of vital records	Relevant plan owner	Plan owner
Changes to draft briefing statements	Relevant plan owner	Plan owner

Figure 16 Typical maintenance changes

Review changes can typically be considered under the following headings:

- business or operational changes
- changes to accommodation
- changes to computer systems and networks
- changes to telecommunications
- changes affecting suppliers
- changes in the perceived risk.

Figure 15 describes typical review changes under each of these headings.

A wide range of maintenance changes can arise depending on the scope and content of the business recovery plans. Figure 16 describes typical maintenance changes.

Whilst responsibility for identifying changes will rest with plan owners, they may need some assistance from the Business Continuity Manager in establishing suitable procedures to identify change within their own business areas. A proactive approach to identifying change will often prove more successful than simply sitting back and waiting for notification of change. Example approaches would include:

- the Business Continuity Manager regularly sending a questionnaire to each plan owner, requesting confirmation that the plans are up to date
- plan owners regularly sending notices to team members to enquire whether there have been any changes which could affect the plan.

Action the changes   Changes will be actioned by the Business Continuity Manager or the plan owner depending on whether it is a review change or a maintenance change.

Review change
The Business Continuity Manager will co-ordinate the actions to implement the change. These actions may involve some or all of the following:

- determine whether the change is likely to alter the potential business impacts that could result from a disruption to business. If so, undertake an impact analysis for the change (ie how the business impacts may change as a result of implementing the change) and identify the minimum requirements for staff, systems, telecommunications etc

- review the recovery objectives to see if they need amending as a result of the change. If a new business process has been added its relative position in the list of either high or low priority processes must be ascertained
- determine whether the change is likely to alter the likelihood of a serious disruption to business. If so, investigate the changed threats and vulnerabilities
- determine whether the existing recovery strategy and stand-by arrangements need to be amended to ensure that recovery objectives can still be met following the proposed change
- determine whether the existing risk reduction measures are sufficient to protect against the changed risks
- if changes are necessary, eg to the existing recovery strategy, stand-by arrangements or risk reduction measures, identify and evaluate options
- review the proposed changes and seek agreement within the central co-ordination team. If necessary seek approval from the top management/executive Board.

Once approval has been given:

- arrange for stand-by or risk reduction measures to be implemented or changed
- update the appropriate business recovery plans and procedures.

Once stand-by or risk reduction measures have been implemented and business continuity plans have been updated ensure that:

- an initial walkthrough test of the changed plan is conducted
- the test programme is amended as necessary
- the awareness/education and assurance programmes are updated as necessary.

Maintenance changes

Maintenance changes will be undertaken by individual plan owners. These may involve some or all of the following actions:

- make any necessary change(s) to task lists

- determine whether any reference information or supporting procedures need to be changed as a result of changes to task lists and, if necessary, make the appropriate changes

- decide whether the changes are likely to need reflecting in other business recovery plans and, if so, inform the appropriate plan owners

- copy details of any changes passed to other plan owners to the Business Continuity Manager so that changes that affect more than one plan can be audited.

Distribute plans and procedures	After plans and procedures have been updated they will need to be distributed to all team members.
	Depending on the extent of the change, updates may be issued in the form of replacement pages or complete new versions.
	All updates should be issued under strict version control with instructions to destroy old versions and guidelines on where and how the plans should be stored.

6.5 Assurance

The final process in the BCM lifecycle involves obtaining assurance that the quality of the BCM deliverables is acceptable to senior business management and that the operational management processes are working satisfactorily.

An audit mechanism will therefore be required by which assurance can be gained that effective tests and reviews are being conducted in line with objectives and programmes.

Confirm maintenance and change control	A similar audit mechanism will be required to ensure that effective change control and plan maintenance is being performed in line with change control procedures.
Receive management acceptance of deliverables	Management acceptance of all deliverables will be required after initial preparation and then after major updates. A management review programme and acceptance criteria will have been documented in the quality plan during Process 1, Initiate Business Continuity Management.

	Issue assurance/ failure report	Each deliverable will either pass or fail its management review and this will be documented in an assurance/ failure report issued to the author of the deliverable. Where deliverables achieve management acceptance, Management Acceptance Certificates can be produced which also specify the latest time by which the deliverable must next be reviewed.
6.6	Key milestones in business continuity management	Within the BCM lifecycle, six key milestones, or levels of maturity, have been identified by which organisations can monitor their progress. These are as follows:

1 Completion of an impact analysis and risk assessment.

2 Definition and agreement of a business continuity strategy.

3 Implementation of stand-by arrangements and risk reduction measures, and the development of business recovery plans.

4 Development and implementation of supporting procedures.

5 A successful initial test of the risk reduction measures, stand-by arrangements and business recovery plans.

6 Establishment of successful management processes to test, review, maintain and audit all BCM deliverables.

Movement from one milestone to the next is a significant step in an organisation's progress with business continuity management, and represents a higher level of confidence in the BCM process.

By the time an organisation reaches level six, it will have a high level of confidence that it can respond effectively to a 'sudden and serious' incident.

Movements between one level and the next tend to be the points at which BCM initiatives falter, as difficulties arise, either in 'moving on' or in maintaining commitment and interest. Only at level six does BCM become an intrinsic and relatively 'subconscious' corporate activity. When this level is reached, it is unlikely that any incident will cause catastrophe or place the organisation at significant risk. The management challenge is then to remain at this level and avoid falling back to an earlier level. Provided that the lifecycle approach is maintained, this problem can successfully be avoided.

7 Skills and techniques

Since BCM is concerned with the survival of the business, the analysis, management and decision making skills of top management will need to be applied throughout the BCM lifecycle. This is most critical during the requirements and strategy stage where key decisions are required on the:

- acceptability of risk
- expenditure on risk reduction and recovery solutions.

Top management skills will, however, also need to be applied to ensure that the BCM strategy is implemented, and then managed, effectively.

The detailed skills and techniques required for business continuity management will vary across the BCM lifecycle.

7.1 Stage 1 – Initiation

Skills
Business continuity management is usually initiated in the form of a project and hence skills in project organisation, control and planning are important.

Techniques
Depending on the size and complexity of the project, project planning techniques such as critical path analysis may be appropriate. Guidance on project organisation, planning and control can be found in the PRINCE Manuals.

7.2 Stage 2 – Requirements and strategy

Skills
The Requirements and strategy stage requires skills in business and technical analysis, evaluation of options and preparation of business cases. Specifically, this requires skills in:

- understanding the organisation's business objectives and business processes, the environment in which the business operates and the organisation's strategies and plans
- understanding the functions and infrastructures that underpin business processes, eg accommodation, computer systems and networks, telecommunications, human resources

- assessing potential business impacts, identifying high priority processes and functions and analysing recovery objectives and minimum requirements

- identifying risks, how they interrelate, their likelihood of occurrence and key vulnerabilities

- identifying and assessing the suitability of risk reduction and recovery options

- drawing conclusions on an effective integrated business continuity strategy and making a persuasive case for its approval by top management.

By its very nature, business continuity management covers all parts of the business and therefore requires a broad understanding of the organisation spanning all critical business processes, technology, human resources etc, as well as knowledge of risk factors and business continuity solutions.

It is unusual to find this combination of skills and experience within a single person and hence Stage 2 of the lifecycle needs to draw on specialist input from many sources. This input will typically be provided via interviews or contributions to working groups.

The project team members will, however, need to demonstrate:

- good understanding of the business and key business processes or an ability to assimilate this information quickly

- good all round understanding of supporting infrastructures; for example, provision of accommodation, office services, IT systems, telecommunications

- knowledge of the methodology to be used and the techniques involved in each stage of the BCM lifecycle; for example, business impact analysis, risk assessment

- ability to command respect and deal with management and staff at all levels.

Again, this breadth of skills is difficult to find but will be critical to the success of the BCM initiative. A situation where the project is dominated by one particular function (for example, IT, office services, sales) at the expense of others must be avoided.

Techniques
The following typical techniques can be used during Stage 2 of the lifecycle:

- interviews, questionnaires, workshops and checklists during business impact analysis and risk assessment
- physical inspections during risk assessment
- checklists of risk reduction and recovery options
- cost benefit analysis.

7.3 Stage 3 – Implementation

Skills
The Implementation stage requires skills in implementation of risk reduction and recovery measures, development of business recovery plans and procedures, and testing. Specifically, this requires skills in:

- establishing management structures for the central co-ordination team and supporting business recovery teams
- defining and allocating responsibilities for BCM from the top management/executive Board down through all levels of the organisation
- developing an effective framework of integrated recovery plans
- specifying, procuring and managing the implementation of risk reduction and recovery solutions
- production of detailed business recovery plans and procedures
- integration of the recovery solutions and business recovery plans and procedures
- initial testing of the strategy and plans.

The first three of these involve essential decision making on structures and responsibility and will require the same broad range of skills as described for the requirements and strategy stage. The remainder involve detailed work in line with the agreed structures and will

IT Infrastructure Library
A Guide to Business Continuity Management

tend to be carried out by specialists across different functions. A wide range of skills will be required each with detailed knowledge in areas such as computer systems and networks, telecommunications, accommodation, personnel and critical business processes. The same overall coordination and integration skills will be required of the project team members as for the requirements and strategy stage.

Techniques
The following typical techniques can be used during stage 3 of the lifecycle:

- proforma frameworks and business recovery plan templates
- interviews, workshops and checklists during the development of detailed business recovery plans.

7.4 Stage 4 – Operational management

Skills
The Operational management stage is an ongoing management discipline as opposed to the project-related work of the previous stages. This requires specific skills in:

- raising and maintaining awareness about BCM
- managing the review, testing, training and audit programmes
- change control.

The operational management processes are likely to be taken on by a Business Continuity Manager who will need to have the experience, credibility and communications skills necessary to keep momentum going once the (often high profile) project has been replaced by ongoing management processes.

Techniques
The following typical techniques can be used during Stage 4 of the lifecycle:

- checklists during the review and testing processes
- various techniques during change control (as described above for Stages 1 to 3 of the lifecycle).

8 Methods and tools

A wide range of methods and tools are available to support the business continuity management lifecycle. However, BCM is a management discipline which requires, amongst other things, decision making, organisation, education and awareness. The approach to these elements of the lifecycle cannot easily be structured into a method or supported by automated tools. Methods and tools play an important part at certain stages of the lifecycle but they only support and do not replace the underlying management processes.

The emphasis in BCM must first be on optimising the underlying processes before selecting methods and tools to support these.

Example
Research at Carnegie Mellon University and the Software Engineering Institute in the USA concluded that an ill-defined process, inconsistent implementation and poor process management are the major limiting factors to the effective use of software technologies.

While there are differences between systems development and BCM similar observations apply:

- the aims and objectives for the process(es) should first be specified
- the process(es) should then be defined and optimised
- where necessary, methods and tools should be selected to support the process or most likely, *parts of the process*.

This process will tend to be where benefits will accrue from:

- a knowledge base to supplement a shortage of skills and experience
- a tried and tested approach
- time and cost savings.

Without first defining and optimising the BCM processes organisations will run the risk of:

- using a flawed approach to BCM resulting in inappropriate, ineffective or un-maintainable strategies and plans
- having a process defined for them by a method or tool vendor which may not suit the organisation.

Each stage of the BCM process requires different skills and techniques and therefore lends itself in different ways to support from a method or tool.

The CCTA IT Infrastructure Library (ITIL) provides guidance on availability management and contingency planning for IT systems across the BCM lifecycle.

8.1 Stage 1 – Initiation

Support for the project organisation, control and planning activities can be provided by the CCTA PRINCE project management method. Automated support tools for PRINCE and other project planning methods are also available from a variety of sources.

The other processes within the Initiation stage – setting policy; specifying terms of reference and scope; and allocating resources do not lend themselves to support from methods or automated tools.

8.2 Stage 2 – Requirements and strategy

Although not always essential, parts of the Requirements and strategy stage can benefit from the use of a method and automated support tool.

Business impact analysis

Business impact analysis involves understanding business processes and assessing the impact that can result from disruption to critical processes. This involves consultation, review of documentation and recording and analysis of information. Support from methods and tools can be provided in the form of:

- checklists of questions to ask
- guidelines for measuring impacts
- facilities for recording and presenting information on business impacts, perhaps in graphical format as illustrated in Figure 2
- facilities for recording information on minimum requirements, perhaps as illustrated in Figures 3 and 4

Chapter 8
Methods and tools

- facilities for presenting different views of minimum requirements; for example, a list of minimum requirements for each individual core team (Figure 4), consolidated requirements for key components such as accommodation, computer systems and networks across all core teams (Figure 5).

Risk assessment

In assessing requirements for business continuity, there are a wide range of different but interrelating risks to consider, from the traditional disasters such as fire and flood through to industrial action, failure of service providers and espionage. Statistical information on incidents is meagre and difficult to interpret and apply to specific problems, thereby making the assessment of risks a largely subjective matter. The risk assessment process can therefore benefit from support from methods and tools in the form of:

- a checklist of risks and factors which may indicate various levels of threat or vulnerability
- **expert** analysis of threat and vulnerability factors to assess overall risks
- facilities for recording and presenting information on threats and vulnerabilities.

Business continuity strategy

The business continuity strategy process involves identification and evaluation of risk reduction and recovery solutions. Methods and tools can assist in:

- identifying recovery options which may be able to satisfy the recovery objectives
- identifying options for reducing risk.

However, a list of options to consider is as much as it is reasonable to expect a method or tool to provide. The suitability of risk reduction and recovery options is very specific to the particular circumstances of each organisation and the activities of evaluating options and defining a business continuity strategy do not lend themselves easily to the formalisation of a method or automated tool.

CRAMM

The CCTA Risk Analysis and Management Method (CRAMM) provides support for the requirements and strategy phase of the business continuity management lifecycle. CRAMM is an automated risk analysis and management tool for IT security and contingency and can be applied to the following components that support the business processes:

- computer systems and networks
- telecommunications equipment and services
- the accommodation used to house equipment and users of computer systems/networks
- critical paper records produced as output from computer systems.

Version 3 of CRAMM has been specifically designed to be consistent with the guidance in this volume and provides all of the functionality described above to support the business impact analysis, risk assessment and business continuity strategy processes.

CRAMM is best used where critical business processes are highly dependent on computer systems and networks, and telecommunications. In such situations, CRAMM will guide the business continuity practitioner through:

- assessment of the impacts on the business process from disruption to computer systems/networks and telecommunications
- assessment of threat and vulnerability levels
- overall assessment of the risks to the business processes
- identification of risk reduction and recovery options.

8.3 Stage 3 – Implementation

Within the Implementation stage, the process 'organisation and implementation planning' does not lend itself easily to support from methods and tools. Varying degrees of support may, however, be required for other implementation processes.

Implementation of stand-by arrangements and risk reduction measures

These processes are concerned with procuring and installing any additional computer systems and networks, telecommunications, accommodation, support services etc that are necessary to meet the requirements of the business continuity strategy. These processes could include, for example, construction of back up accommodation and computer facilities or taking a contract with a provider of commercial recovery services. Depending on the size and complexity of the implementation required, support from methods and tools may be required for:

- project planning, organisation and control
- specification of requirements
- procurement
- development or enhancements to computer software.

The CCTA methods PRINCE, SSADM (Structured Systems Analysis and Development Method) and TAP (Total Acquisition Process) provide support in these areas.

Development of business recovery plans and procedures

The development and maintenance of business recovery plans and procedures is the area in which methods and, in particular, software support tools tend to be most useful for business continuity management. The majority of specialist business continuity or contingency planning tools provide support to these processes.

The requirements for support emanate from the following characteristics of the recovery planning process:

- the need to produce and maintain an integrated set of business continuity plans, some of which will need to hold common or related information
- the need to record and manipulate large volumes of text and reference data
- the need to ensure that plans are complete and consistent
- the need to record and manipulate reference data that may already be held on other computer systems; for example, staff records, asset registers.

Typical recovery planning tools will provide some or all of the following functions:

- development and maintenance of an integrated set of plans with common information that is required across more than one plan only having to be entered, or amended, in one place
- example recovery plan templates and the ability to tailor these

- flexible reporting, eg the ability to print a complete set of plans, individual plans, the parts of a plan that relate to a specific incident

- flexible searching and sorting facilities for reference data

- facilities to import and export information from and to other tools.

Used effectively, recovery tools can provide improved consistency between plans throughout an organisation. The underlying templates and knowledge bases help to ensure that all necessary aspects of the plan are covered and that time and cost savings during production and maintenance are realised.

It is important, however, that tools should support the recovery planning process and not drive it. A framework of business recovery plans should be produced and the optimum structure of individual plans defined before decisions are taken on whether tools are required. An organisation may, for example, decide that its plans are best produced and maintained by making use of its standard PC software tools, eg word processing, spreadsheet, database.

The use of a specialist recovery planning tool will have implications for the way in which the plans will be maintained. Recovery planning tools usually require specialist training and those involved in plan maintenance will need to be trained. If plan ownership and the responsibility for maintenance have been devolved to individual business functions, this could mean that significant numbers of people need to be trained or, alternatively, that a centralised approach to maintenance should be adopted.

Initial testing

The process of testing does not lend itself easily to support from methods and tools although checklists and proformas may be of use in developing test plans. Also, some recovery planning tools are flexible enough to be used interactively during an incident. This means that rather than just using such a tool to produce paper copies of plans for later reference during an incident, the tool can be used to generate relevant parts of the plans at the time, for example, all elements relating to a particular business function or a particular floor of the building. In this respect recovery planning tools can also provide support to the testing processes.

8.4 Stage 4 – Operational management

The education and awareness and training processes may be supported in part by computer based packages. As with testing, recovery planning tools may provide some support with education and awareness.

The review, change control and assurance processes are involved with changes or auditing relating to BCM deliverables produced in earlier stages of the lifecycle. Tools used in Stages 1 to 3 will therefore continue to have a role during Stage 4. The support provided to change control by recovery planning tools can be an important factor in the establishment of successful operational management for BCM.

9 Common applications of BCM

The processes within the BCM lifecycle are generic and apply to a wide range of situations. This chapter highlights particular issues that may need to be considered for the following common applications of BCM:

- where business processes are centralised or there is a high dependency on centralised IT services
- where business processes are distributed across more than one geographic location or there is a high dependency on distributed IT services and networks
- where there is a high dependency on telecommunications or other services provided by third parties outside the direct control of the organisation
- where business functions or processes have been, or are being, outsourced.

The issues relating to each common application are considered under the following headings:

- terms of reference and scope
- business impact analysis
- risk assessment
- risk reduction options
- recovery options
- evaluation of options
- command control and communications structure
- framework for business recovery plans
- implementation of stand-by and risk reduction solutions
- development of business recovery plans
- operational management.

Owing to the wide diversity within different applications of BCM the issues described in this section

IT Infrastructure Library
A Guide to Business Continuity Management

are designed to be thought-provoking rather than, necessarily, comprehensive. They should prove useful where BCM is being introduced to organisations which are operating in similar environments.

9.1 Centralised environment

For the purposes of this guide, a centralised environment is considered to be one in which critical business processes and their components, such as computer systems, are concentrated in a single geographic location. The organisation may or may not have access to alternative accommodation and services for recovery purposes. The ultimate centralised environment is one in which all business processes are operated from a single location.

Terms of reference and scope

The terms of reference will be broadly as described in Chapter 3. The scope of the BCM initiative could cover all of the risks described on Figure 6, although particular attention will need to be given to physical risks relating to the single location.

Business impact analysis

In a centralised environment, a major incident affecting the single location or the supply of services to the single location will immediately halt the business processes performed from that location. Unlike distributed environments, where business processes may be supported from several locations, the impact on centralised processes will often be total rather than partial. The major issue for centralised environments therefore often relates to the speed with which business processes need to be recovered at alternative locations.

Where business processes are closely integrated and rely on shared components, such as computer systems (which is often the case in centralised environments) recovery options may be constrained by the need to fall back to a similar centralised environment. In these circumstances, it is particularly important that the business impact analysis accurately establishes the recovery objectives and minimum requirements for each business process.

Risk assessment

Since the single centralised location represents a massive single point of failure for the organisation particular attention will need to be paid to the risks of:

- damage or denial of access to the premises and the computer systems, paper records and other assets located within it

Chapter 9
Common applications of BCM

- loss of power to the location
- loss of telecommunications services to the location
- industrial action affecting the location.

Because of the single point of failure, centralised organisations will tend to be more vulnerable to physical incidents affecting the premises than distributed organisations. Even relatively minor incidents, such as a localised fire, affecting one process can cause wide disruption to many other processes if, as a result, access to the premises is denied.

- Care should also be taken to identify whether there are critical single points of failure relating to services provided to the location, eg:
  - all telecommunications to the site (even where different service providers are involved) being routed through a single exchange, cable route or access point to the building
  - all power to the site being provided via a single substation, cable route or access point to the building
  - a single access route to the location which could be blocked by adverse weather conditions, accident, industrial action etc.

Ultimately, it may not be feasible to remove such single points of failure but their existence will need to be recognised during consideration of risk reduction and recovery options.

Risk reduction options

Where possible, options for avoiding single points of failure and reducing the dependence on a single location should be considered, for example splitting business processes across more than one site. In many cases, however, this will not be viable for financial, technical or other business reasons. In this event, risk reduction options, such as the examples provided in Chapter 4, should be given a high priority. In particular, the following should be considered:

- control over physical access to the premises
- fire, flood and bomb protection
- physical protection of incoming services
- protection of vital electronic and manual media

- reducing the dependence on staff located at the site.

Care should also be taken to ensure that the design and layout of the site are as resilient as possible to partial failures or disasters. With a poorly designed site, even a relatively minor incident may result in widespread disruption to all business processes. Conversely, if localised incidents can be contained then the impact may be limited to those processes that are directly affected. Options for providing internal resilience within a site include:

- multiple access routes

- taking care over the location of staff, computer systems and other components of business processes to reduce the risk of critical processes all being affected by the same localised incident

- providing alternative cable routes for computer networks, telecommunications and power

- compartmentalising the building to make it easier to contain an incident within a defined area.

Risk reduction options for critical services include:

- distributing services across more than one service provider

- distributing power and telecommunications services across alternative cable routes and building access points

- using alternative technologies, eg wireless based communications services as an alternative to cable based services.

Recovery options

With a centralised environment, the worst case scenario is often the destruction or denial of access to the single site, perhaps as a result of fire, flood, explosion etc. Such incidents may render the site, or at least part of it, inoperable for considerable periods of time. Unless total dependence is placed on risk reduction measures and insurance, which in itself is a high risk strategy, some form of planning to recover at alternative premises will be required. This will involve:

- stand-by accommodation, possibly pre-equipped with furniture, power and telecommunications cabling

Chapter 9
Common applications of BCM

- arrangements for computer systems and networks to be recovered and made available to the stand-by site
- off-site back up for data, vital records and other critical assets which may remain isolated within the affected site.

Fully equipped stand-by sites are very expensive and can only be justified where the potential impacts and risks to the business are very high. A trade-off usually has to be struck between the speed at which business processes can be recovered at the stand-by site and the cost of pre-equipping the stand-by accommodation.

It can be expensive and complex to establish plans for the rapid movement of large numbers of staff to alternative accommodation. To achieve a cost-effective recovery strategy, there may be a need for some recovery objectives to be relaxed. Facilities for core teams may also need to be pared down to the absolute minimum. Indeed, for centralised environments, business activities may have to be downsized for a considerable period until a full recovery can be effected.

Recovery options for a partial disaster will need to be considered and may, typically, include pre-equipping conference rooms, staff restaurants and other areas with cabling and stand-by equipment.

Evaluation of options

Options for centralised organisations will be more constrained than for distributed organisations as a result of:

- having to recover entire business processes, groups of integrated processes or, ultimately, the entire organisation
- the non-availability of alternative stand-by arrangements and communications facilities within the organisation.

These factors will tend to result in the organisation having to place a heavy reliance during invocation on providers of external services and other third parties outside the direct control of the organisation. This will, in turn have implications for the costs, ability to meet recovery objectives and business risks associated with each option.

Command control and communications structure	Effective recovery from an incident is dependent on making the correct decisions quickly. In a centralised environment, there is a greater risk that key decision makers may have been caught up in the incident. The command and control structure should therefore place a high priority on being able to cope with unavailability of key staff.
	With a total disaster at a single centralised site, the difficulties of communicating with staff can be exacerbated. This contrasts with a distributed environment where staff may be able to communicate via an alternative unaffected location. The communications structure should pay careful attention to the means by which information will be distributed to staff.
Framework for business recovery plans	The framework for business recovery plans is likely to be similar to that described in Figure 12.
Implementation of stand-by and risk reduction solutions	Most of the issues to consider during implementation will be similar to those associated with other scenarios, although particular attention should be paid to telecommunications. Unlike distributed scenarios where there may be options to divert communications from one site to another this may not be possible in a centralised environment.
	The stand-by arrangements may need to be used for some considerable time until the original site has been refurbished or alternative permanent accommodation has been prepared.
	In the worst case of a total disaster, the whole site may have been lost and careful consideration will need to be given to how the central co-ordination team and business recovery teams will communicate and where they will be located.
Development of business recovery plans	The issues involved in developing business recovery plans for centralised environments will be similar to those described in Chapter 5. Particular care will need to be taken to ensure that: • the plans can still be invoked even where key staff are unavailable • effective communications are put in place to ensure that staff can be contacted in a controlled manner in the immediate aftermath of an incident

Chapter 9
Common applications of BCM

- communications can be maintained at stand-by facilities, particularly where the previously centralised environment may now be distributed across multiple locations.

In centralised environments, key information and assets concentrated in the single site may have been damaged or be inaccessible in the immediate aftermath of an incident. The recovery strategy will have put heavy emphasis on appropriate back up procedures and the business recovery plans will need to pay careful attention to the actions necessary to recover and restore information, and where possible to salvage critical assets.

Operational management

The issues involved in the operational management of business continuity for centralised environments will be similar to those described in Chapter 6. Owing to the nature of centralised environments it may not be feasible to carry out full tests on the organisation's response to its greatest risk, that of destruction or denial of access to the single site. The business risks involved in undertaking a full test are likely, in most cases, to be too great and reliance will have to be placed on tests of technical components or business components. Where the test programme is based around a series of tests of individual components care must be taken to ensure that, in the event of a full invocation, a co-ordinated recovery of all components can be achieved.

9.2 Distributed environment

For the purposes of this guide, a distributed environment is considered to be one in which critical business processes and their components, such as computer systems, are distributed across two or more geographic locations which are not both at risk from the same disaster or incident.

Terms of reference and scope

The terms of reference will be broadly as described in Chapter 3. The scope of the BCM initiative could cover all of the risks described on Figure 6. Whilst business processes may be intrinsically less vulnerable to physical disaster, they tend to rely heavily on the communications and transport services that link the multiple locations together. Particular attention may, therefore, need to be paid to the risks relating to these services, particularly where they are provided by third parties.

In setting the scope for BCM in a distributed environment there may be a temptation to limit the scope to individual sites which are perceived to be at high risk, or to apply BCM on a site by site basis. This is dangerous because it will not allow the risks and opportunities presented by the environment to be fully explored. The scope of the exercise should be defined by the business processes to be covered and not by geographic location since:

- a broader perspective of the whole business can be taken
- interdependencies between the components of business processes that are distributed across multiple sites can be identified and addressed
- additional recovery options may be identified
- the cost of risk reduction and recovery solutions may be reduced or shared.

Ultimately, there is a significant risk that, if all components of the business process are not addressed together, at least until the end of the requirements and strategy stage, the business process will still fail even though individual components may have been recovered. Once a strategy has been set for the business processes within the scope of the exercise, a co-ordinated phased approach to implementation may be introduced across the multiple sites.

Business impact analysis

In a distributed environment, disasters or other physical incidents will only affect part of the business process. If the affected components are critical then the impacts will still be very high and it is therefore important to understand the degree to which the processes depend on these components.

The business impact analysis will therefore need to investigate the degree of dependence and establish recovery objectives and minimum requirements for the individual components.

Risk assessment

In a distributed environment, business processes may be resilient to physical disasters and incidents at individual sites. However, the nature of the distributed environment is likely to mean that business processes are highly dependent on the communications between sites. The following risks will therefore need to be examined closely:

- loss of computer network services

Chapter 9
Common applications of BCM

- loss of telecommunications services
- loss of transport services between sites.

Where distributed business processes are highly automated and reliant on networked computer systems, further security related risks may be introduced. The security of computer networks is only as strong as the weakest link and vulnerabilities at one site may be exploited to the detriment of other, apparently well protected, sites. Examples will include:

- the introduction of a computer virus or other malicious software which could rapidly infect the entire network
- a hacker gaining access at one site through lax security procedures and from there infiltrating other systems and network nodes.

With the rapid increase in the use of public networking services, such as the Internet, the above risks are very real and a distributed environment could therefore be disrupted very rapidly unless suitable controls and procedures are put in place. Similar concerns will exist with centralised environments that use external network services, but it is often easier for a centralised environment to implement a common security policy.

Where the sites in a distributed environment are spread across different countries additional risks may be introduced as a result of the different legislative systems. Public networks such as the Internet are completely unregulated and many countries do not have equivalents of the United Kingdom's computer misuse and data protection legislation. In the absence of international copyright legislation, organisations putting proprietary material onto public networks run the risk of unauthorised copying and distribution.

Risk reduction options

A suitable range of risk reduction options will need to be implemented at each site to protect against risks such as damage or denial of access to the premises, and unavailability of key staff.

The nature of the distributed environment should be exploited as far as possible to build resilience into the business process. This could involve distributing key staff, computer systems, data, vital records and other critical assets across multiple sites.

IT Infrastructure Library
A Guide to Business Continuity Management

Particular care should be taken to reduce the risks relating to communications between sites and the following measures should be considered:

- development and implementation of a co-ordinated network security policy across all sites

- distributing computer network and telecommunications services across more than one service provider, and across alternative cable routes and building access points

- using alternative technologies, eg wireless based communications services as an alternative to cable based services.

Recovery options

A distributed environment will usually allow for more recovery options than a centralised environment. For example, in the event of a disaster at one site, the following options may be available:

- relocate key staff and salvaged equipment to an alternative site

- divert computer network and telecommunications services to an alternative site

- make use of computer systems already established at the alternative site.

If critical electronic data and vital paper records have been distributed across different sites, and alternative accommodation, systems and telecommunications services can be provided quickly for key staff, then it may be possible to limit the disruption to an absolute minimum.

It may be possible to interrogate computer systems at the affected site via a distributed network even when physical access to the site is not possible.

Evaluation of options

Recovery of staff from one site to another within a distributed environment will usually mean that some (non-critical) staff at the receiving site will need to be displaced. The following issues should be considered when evaluating options within a distributed environment:

- the extent of the impact at the receiving site – will it precipitate a second crisis within the organisation?

Chapter 9
Common applications of BCM

- the time for which the receiving site could cope without there being serious secondary impacts on the business

- the compatibility of equipment across sites – in a distributed environment there can be significant differences in system configuration and compatibility between apparently similar sites

- whether staff can be relocated easily to the receiving site, and for how long

- whether the security facilities at the receiving site match those required by the affected site

- whether the facilities at the receiving site can be upgraded to support the whole operation for an extended period.

Command, control and communications structure

The command and control structure will need to include representatives from the receiving site as well as from the affected site. Business recovery teams will need to be established at the receiving site to prepare accommodation, reconfigure computer systems and networks, restore data, divert telecommunications etc and these will need to be integrated with those teams involved with damage assessment and salvage at the affected site.

All key components of the business processes affected will need to be represented in the command, control and communications structure and this may involve additional sites not directly affected by the incident. Effective communications between all parts of the business will be required to facilitate a smooth recovery process. One of the unaffected sites can act as a hub for communications with staff, customers, key suppliers, the media and other interested parties.

A co-ordinated approach to crisis management and public relations will be essential to avoid giving an impression of chaos. This is particularly important where business reacts quickly on the basis of rumour. For example, in international financial markets, misinterpretation of an incident in the UK could be blown out of proportion by staff in other countries reacting to rumour.

Framework for business recovery plans	The basic framework for the business recovery plans will be similar to that described in Chapter 5 although more plans are likely to be needed to cover the actions required at both the affected and the receiving sites. An essential component of the plans will be how they facilitate communications.
	Rapid recovery at the receiving site will only be possible if the systems, networks and other assets used by the two sites remain compatible. The ability to co-ordinate change control easily between the sites involved will therefore be an important consideration in the design of the framework.
	Often in a distributed environment, sites will provide reciprocal back up to each other. To ease maintenance and change control, all business recovery plans should be developed to common standards set out in the framework.
Implementation of stand-by and risk reduction solutions	Since distributed environments often contain an inherent degree of resilience to failure or disruption, it is likely that this will be further exploited by the risk reduction and recovery strategy. The risk reduction strategy will aim to reduce single points of failure and the recovery strategy will seek to make use of alternative accommodation, systems, telecommunications and other assets within the business process.
	The implementation of stand-by and risk reduction solutions may therefore involve making adjustments to the business process or its supporting components. There is, however, a danger that internal solutions tend to be treated in a less formal way than external contractual arrangements. Strong project management will be required to ensure that solutions are implemented effectively and in accordance with the strategy.
	Without close monitoring, internal changes in the business process or its underlying components can easily go unnoticed and thereby invalidate the strategy. Careful monitoring of any internal or reciprocal arrangements will therefore be critical to the success of the overall business continuity strategy.

Chapter 9
Common applications of BCM

Development of business recovery plans	The issues involved in developing business recovery plans for distributed environments will be similar to those described in Chapter 5. Particular care will need to be taken to ensure that the following information is held:

- accurate contact and access arrangements between sites, as emergency access may be required to the receiving site outside normal working hours
- details of the high priority functions and core teams to be moved to the receiving site
- details of the low priority functions at the receiving site that will be displaced by the incoming core teams, as critical time can be lost in resolving disputes over relative priorities
- configuration details and lists of assets required by the incoming core teams
- detailed procedures for diverting communications, recovering and distributing vital records and restoring data on computer systems.

Operational management	As already described, maintenance and change control are particularly important elements if high levels of business continuity are to be achieved in a distributed environment. Contact details, asset inventories, configuration details and procedures must all be kept up to date and this may not be easy when each site is facing its own business pressures.
	Education, training and testing will also be very important to ensure that the sites involved can co-operate and work together effectively. The potential risks in relying on apparently compatible equipment at the receiving site must be eliminated through rigorous technical testing. Testing can become complex where several sites are involved and demands a higher degree of planning. The timescales and costs involved in testing may also be significant.

9.3 Outsourced functions or processes including dependency on external services

Some organisations are highly dependent on external services, the provision of which is outside their direct control, eg telecommunications, power, information, distribution, raw materials etc.

The issues associated with managing the continuity of these external services are very similar to those met when business processes are outsourced, so references in this section to outsourced business functions apply equally to the use of external services.

Over recent years, many organisations have outsourced business functions or even entire business processes, typically for the following reasons:

- to save costs
- to improve service levels
- to allow the organisation to concentrate on core business processes.

The distinction between the outsourcing of business functions (such as IT) and business processes (such as customer services and accounting) is important. Where entire business processes have been outsourced the organisation will be entirely dependent on the service provider for operation and recovery of the process. Where business functions or other components of the business process have been outsourced, the organisation will be partially dependent on the service provider for recovery of the process. This is not to say, however, that the organisation will be any less vulnerable since the outsourced component may be highly critical to the process. Furthermore, recovery of partially outsourced business processes will require careful co-ordination between the customer and the service provider.

Terms of reference and scope

While a provider of outsourced services will be responsible for providing a service in accordance with agreed service levels, the customer must take overall responsibility for continuity of the business. Although compensation may be available from the service provider where service levels have not been met, this will be of little consequence if the customer is dead.

Consideration will need to be given to the extent to which detailed investigations will need to be undertaken in relation to individual service providers and this will relate to the perceived criticality of the outsourced service. Where resilience is available through the existence of several service providers, eg several distributors, it may be sufficient to require each provider to develop and implement their own business continuity strategy whilst ensuring that suitable stand-by arrangements are available in the event that one of the providers fails. On the other hand, where an outsourced service represents a critical single point of failure, detailed investigations by the customer may be justified.

Chapter 9
Common applications of BCM

Where outsourced services are highly critical to the organisation, representatives of the service provider can be incorporated on to the steering committee and project team.

Business impact analysis

If the continuity of business processes is critical to an organisation then the impacts from a disruption to these processes will be severe, regardless of how the processes are provided. The overall impact from disruption to business processes is therefore unlikely to differ depending on whether or not processes have been outsourced.

Where components of business processes are being outsourced it is, however, important that the degree of dependence on the service provider is understood. It is recommended that where processes are being outsourced, a business impact analysis is undertaken specifically to investigate the impacts that could result from a disruption affecting the outsourced services. This will enable recovery objectives and minimum requirements to be identified which can then be incorporated into service level agreements.

Risk assessment

Where business functions or processes have been outsourced, very careful attention will need to be paid to the risk that the service provider will fail to perform, perhaps as a result of:

- a disaster or denial of access at the provider's premises
- failure of the provider's critical computer systems, networks or other assets
- industrial action
- commercial failure, eg insolvency
- poor performance through untrained or over stretched staff, weak management or similar problems.

The risk assessment will involve refinement and extension of the above list of risks and assessment of levels of threat and vulnerability.

Certain risks relating to service providers may be difficult to assess by the customer, eg:

- industrial action
- commercial failure

- training and motivation of the service provider's staff

- conflicts of interest with other customers of the service provider.

In such cases, the customer will need to take a pragmatic view based on the information that is available.

While attention might be focused on the risks relating to availability and service levels associated with the outsourced service, care should also be taken to ensure that the outsourced service does not introduce additional risks such as:

- loss of confidentiality, eg unauthorised disclosure of sensitive information, perhaps as a result of hacking or other infiltration of computer systems via the service provider's network

- loss of integrity, eg through the introduction of computer viruses or other malicious software.

These may also form part of the risk assessment.

In assessing levels of risks, the following issues should also be considered:

- a service provider may have many other customers to support and in a disaster there may be significant pressure brought to bear by larger customers, so it is important that relative priorities are understood

- risk reduction and recovery solutions to support one customer of the service provider may not suit another

- the strength or weakness of the provider's security policies will change the risk profile of the customer; for example, a disgruntled employee of the service provider could become a direct threat to the customer, or a hacker may exploit weaknesses in the security of the provider to attack the customer

- the provider may have other customers that are direct targets, eg they may be providing services to a pharmaceutical company which is at risk from animal rights activists.

Chapter 9
Common applications of BCM

A BCM risk assessment can make a valuable contribution during the evaluation of whether to outsource business functions or processes and, if so, to which service provider(s).

Risk reduction options

Depending on the nature of the business processes and functions being outsourced, the following options can be used, where appropriate, to reduce the risk:

- as part of the evaluation criteria for selecting the service provider, stipulate that resilience should be provided by distributing key components of the business process or function across several sites
- require service providers to develop and implement business continuity and security strategies
- require the service providers to demonstrate that the BCM plans have been developed and are regularly and adequately tested
- ensure that the highest risks, or risks that are difficult to assess, are specifically addressed in the contract and service level agreements
- consider the possibility of splitting the outsourced functions and processes across more than one provider
- ensure that a suitable infrastructure is in place to facilitate all communications with the service provider
- second customer staff to the service provider to assist in the management of business continuity
- pre-establish the level of priority to be given to the customer in the event of a disaster or other incident
- use service providers that do not have other high risk customers
- in extremis, only outsource non-critical business functions and processes.

Where appropriate, risk reduction measures should be incorporated into the contract and service level agreements.

Recovery options	Most of the recovery options described in Chapter 4 can be considered. Service level agreements should specify the recovery objectives and minimum requirements derived from the business impact analysis. Other recovery options may include: • providing in-house back up facilities for the outsourced services • arranging a business continuity recovery contract with a second outsourcing organisation, possibly a competitor involved in the original procurement competition • using the provider to provide stand-by facilities for other business functions and processes that have not been outsourced.
Evaluation of options	Evaluation of options should include assessment of the following: • the ability of the provider to meet the recovery requirements, both in the short- and long-term • whether the implementation of recovery options will constrain future business and technical strategies • the level of commitment given to BCM by the service provider • the allocation of cost between the service provider and the customer • whether the options can accommodate future growth in the customer's business and the associated business continuity requirements.
Command, control and communications structure	Where appropriate, representatives of the customer should be included as part of the provider's command and control structure and vice versa. Alternatively, special liaison teams may need to be established. The responsibilities and levels of authority should be clearly defined and agreed.
Framework for business recovery plans	The framework for business recovery plans may be similar to that described in Figure 12 but extended to include plans relating to individual service providers.

Chapter 9
Common applications of BCM

Implementation of stand-by and risk reduction solutions	The following issues should be considered during implementation of stand-by and recovery solutions:

- the location of the emergency control centre and its accessibility by representatives of both the customer and the service provider
- ownership of risk reduction and stand-by equipment
- any changes that will be required to existing procedures, eg for taking back-ups, protection of vital records
- whether there is a need to install specialist telecommunications, or other, equipment.

Development of business recovery plans	The following issues should be considered during development of business recovery plans:

- the allocation of tasks between the service provider's and customer's staff
- the need for change control to cater for changes at both organisations
- the time required for travelling between the sites
- the need for the customer to implement adequate audit procedures when recovery is taking place to allow additional expenditure to be audited
- how salvaged material will be protected at the service provider's premises, particularly where confidentiality is important
- how crisis management and public relations will be co-ordinated.

Operational management	Responsibilities for testing should be carefully defined and the frequency and type of tests required from service providers should be well documented and form part of the contract. The provider should, where possible, be contractually obliged to rectify any omissions or weaknesses that are identified during testing and to do so within set timescales.
	There should also be opportunities for representatives of the customer to witness tests undertaken by the service provider. The customer should be involved in setting the test objectives and scenarios.

Testing can be an expensive element of business continuity and if not managed effectively costs can escalate rapidly. The allocation of costs for testing should be identified and agreed as part of the contract. This may also include penalties for failure to test, as well as for tests that are delayed, do not work, or have to be repeated.

All types of tests should place a high priority on how well communications between the customer and service provider work.

Education, awareness and training on business continuity policy, strategies and plans will be essential for the service provider in meeting its business continuity obligations and again should be defined as part of the contract. Depending on the nature of the business processes and functions careful consideration should be given to the confidentiality of information provided during training.

Change management procedures should be structured to take account of changes within the service provider as well as at the customer. The service provider should not be able to make significant changes to the business continuity strategy or plans without prior written agreement.

The contract should make allowance for assurance checks on the service provider and these should be incorporated into the customer's audit plans and procedures.

Bibliography

CCTA guidance

CCTA is responsible for promoting the effective use of information systems in central government. It publishes a wide range of advice and guidance on issues of strategic importance that could affect the business and organisation of departments.

The following CCTA, and other, publications provide further information on topics covered in this guide.

Management of Risk Library

The Management of Risk Library volumes are available from HMSO, through its bookshops and agents, as detailed on the back cover of this book.

- Introduction to the Management of Risk
  ISBN 0 11 330648 2

- Management of Programme Risk
  ISBN 0 11 330672 5

- Management of Project Risk
  ISBN 0 11 330636 9

- An Introduction to Managing Project Risk
  ISBN 0 11 330671 7

- Management of Risk – Case Study 1
  ISBN 0 11 330667 9

Programme and Project Management Library

The Programme and Project Management volumes are available from HMSO, through its bookshops and agents, as detailed on the back cover of this book.

- An Introduction to Programme Management
  ISBN 0 11 330611 3

- Guide to Programme Management
  ISBN 0 11 330600 8

- PRINCE User's Guide to CRAMM
  ISBN 0 11 330596 6

IT Infrastructure Library	The IT Infrastructure Library Guides are available from ITIMF Ltd, at 1a Taverners Square, Silver Road, Norwich NR3 4SY
	• Contingency Planning ISBN 0 11 330524 9
	• Availability Management ISBN 0 11 330551 6
	• Change Management ISBN 0 11 330525 7
	• Configuration Management ISBN 0 11 330530 3
	• An Introduction to Business Continuity Management ISBN 0 11 330669 5
Procurement Guides	The TAP Guides are available from HMSO, through its bookshops and agents, as detailed on the back cover of this book.
	• TAP Systems Guide ISBN 0 11 330840 X
	• TAP Services Guide ISBN 0 11 330839 6
PRINCE documentation	The PRINCE Reference Manuals (a set of five guides) are published by NCC Blackwell and are available from NCC Blackwell Ltd, Oxford House, Oxford Road, Manchester M1 7ED.
	• PRINCE Manuals ISBN 1 85554 012 6
Quality Management Library	The CCTA Quality Management Library is available as a set of five volumes from HMSO, through its bookshops and agents, as detailed on the back cover of this book.
	• Quality Management Library ISBN 0 11 330569 9

Bibliography

Other CCTA documentation The following volumes are available from HMSO, through its bookshops and agents, as detailed on the back cover of this book.

- BPR (Business Process Re-engineering) in the Public Sector
  ISBN 011 330651 2

- Guidelines for Directing Information Technology Security
  ISBN 0 946683 33 6

Other publications The following can be obtained free of charge from CCTA Library on 01603 704930.

- Management briefing: Safeguarding the Business – The Role of Business Continuity Management

- An Overview of CRAMM

Survive! Magazine – Publisher, the Survive! Secretariat, The Chapel, Royal Victoria Patriotic Building, Fitzhugh Grove, London SW18 3SX, Tel: 0181 874 6266, Fax: 0181 874 6446.

BS7799, 1995 A Code of Practice for Information Security Management.

Professional Development The Business Continuity Institute (BCI), an industry independent body, has been set up to provide an independently moderated and internationally recognised accreditation and certification scheme for business continuity professionals. Anyone wanting more information about the scheme should contact the institute at PO Box 4474, London SW18 3XB.

Glossary

ACD	Automatic Call Distribution.
ALE	Annual Loss Expectancy, a technique for evaluating business continuity solutions.
Alert phase	The first phase of a business recovery plan in which initial emergency procedures and damage assessments are activated.
Asset	Component of a business process. Assets can include people, accommodation, computer systems, networks, paper records, fax machines etc.
Assurance	The processes by which an organisation can verify the accuracy and completeness of its BCM plans.
BCM	Business Continuity Management.
BCM activity	An action or series of actions as part of a BCM process.
BCM lifecycle	The complete set of activities and processes necessary to manage business continuity – divided into four stages.
BCM process	A set of activities with defined deliverables forming a discrete part of the BCM lifecycle.
BS7799	BSI standard on the management of information security.
Business function	A business unit within an organisation, eg a department, division, branch.
Business process	A group of business activities undertaken by an organisation in pursuit of a common goal. Typical business processes include receiving orders, marketing services, selling products, delivering services, distributing products, invoicing for services, accounting for money received. A business process will usually depend on several business functions for support, eg IT, personnel, accommodation. A business process will rarely operate in isolation, ie other business processes will depend on it and it will depend on other processes.

Business recovery objective	The desired time within which business processes should be recovered, and the minimum staff, assets and services required within this time.
Business recovery plans	Documents describing the roles, responsibilities and actions necessary to resume business processes following a business disruption.
Business recovery plan framework	A template business recovery plan (or set of plans) produced to allow the structure and proposed contents to be agreed before the detailed business recovery plan is produced.
Business recovery team	A defined group of personnel with a defined role and subordinate range of actions to facilitate recovery of a business function or process.
CCTA	The Government Centre for Information Systems.
Central co-ordination team	The team that will provide overall co-ordination and control during recovery from an incident, typically comprising managers at one level below the top management/executive Board.
Command, control and communications	The processes by which an organisation retains overall co-ordination of its recovery effort during invocation of business recovery plans.
Contingency planning	Planning to address unwanted occurrences that may happen at a later time. Traditionally, the term has been used to refer to planning for the recovery of IT systems rather than entire business processes.
CRAMM	CCTA Risk Analysis and Management Method used to identify and justify all the necessary protective measures to ensure the security of both current and future IT systems used for processing valuable or sensitive data.
Crisis management	The processes by which an organisation manages the wider impact of a disaster, such as adverse media coverage.
Damage assessment	Assessment of the damage to the organisation's assets, to assist in deciding whether to invoke stand-by arrangements, to identify assets that can be salvaged etc.

Glossary

Dependency	The reliance, either direct or indirect, of one process or activity upon another.
Disaster recovery planning	A series of processes that focus only upon the recovery processes, principally in response to physical disasters, that are contained within BCM.
Emergency Response	The initial response to an incident, focused on protecting human life and the organisation's assets.
Impact scenario	Description of the type of impact on the business that could follow a business disruption. Will usually be related to a business process and will always refer to a period of time, eg customer services will be unable to operate for two days.
Intelligent customer	The purchaser (as distinct from the provider) of sophisticated services. The term is often used in relation to the outsourcing of IT/IS.
Invocation (of business recovery plans)	Putting business recovery plans into operation after a business disruption.
Invocation (of stand-by arrangements)	Putting stand-by arrangements into operation as part of business recovery activities.
Invocation and recovery phase	The second phase of a business recovery plan.
IS	Information Systems
IT	Information Technology
ITIL	The CCTA IT Infrastructure Library – a set of guides on the management and provision of operational IT services.
Master plan	A business recovery plan which supports overall coordination and control of the recovery effort. Used by the central co-ordination team.
Maturity level/ milestone	The degree to which BCM activities and processes have become standard business practice within an organisation.
Outsourcing	The process by which functions performed by the organisation are contracted out for operation, on the organisation's behalf, by third parties.

PABX	Private Automatic Branch Exchange.
Programme	A collection of activities and projects that collectively implement a new corporate requirement or function.
PRINCE	**PR**ojects **IN** a **C**ontrolled **E**nvironment, the CCTA project management method.
Reference data	Information that supports the plans and action lists, such as names and addresses or inventories, which is indexed within the plan.
Return to normal phase	The phase within a business recovery plan which re-establishes normal operations.
Risk	A measure of the exposure to which an organisation may be subjected. This is a combination of the likelihood of a business disruption occurring and the possible loss that may result from such business disruption.
Risk reduction measure	Measures taken to reduce the likelihood of a business disruption occurring (as opposed to planning to recover after a disruption).
Salvage	Recovery and restoration of damaged assets, as opposed to replacement.
Self-insurance	A decision to bear the losses that could result from a disruption to the business as opposed to taking insurance cover on the risk.
Service level agreement	A formal statement of service characteristics between a demander and supplier of services.
Service provider	A third party organisation supplying services or products to customers.
SSADM	Structured Systems Analysis and Design Method, owned by CCTA but publicly documented and available for use by all. SSADM is a standard method for analysis and design in software development projects.
Stand-by arrangements	Arrangements to have available assets which have been identified as replacements should primary assets be unavailable following a business disruption. Typically includes accommodation, computer systems and networks, telecommunications and sometimes people.

TAP   Total Acquisition Process, the CCTA approach to the procurement of IS products and services.

Task lists   Defined tasks, allocated to recovery teams and individuals, within a phase of a plan. These are supported by reference data.

IT Infrastructure Library
A Guide to Business Continuity Management

A List of activities by process

Stage 1
Initiation

Process 1 – Initiation
Activities
1.1   Set policy
1.2   Specify terms of reference and scope
1.3   Allocate resources
1.4   Define project organisation and control structure
1.5   Agree project and quality plans

Stage 2
Requirements and strategy

Process 2 – Perform business impact analysis
Activities
2.1   Identify business processes
2.2   Define impact scenarios
2.3   Measure potential business impacts
2.4   Define business recovery objectives
2.5   Assess minimum requirements

Process 3 – Perform risk assessment
Activities
3.1   Identify risks
3.2   Assess threat and vulnerability levels
3.3   Assess levels of risk

Process 4 – Develop business continuity strategy
Activities
4.1   Identify and evaluate recovery options
4.2   Identify and evaluate risk reduction options
4.3   Define overall strategy

IT Infrastructure Library
A Guide to Business Continuity Management

Stage 3
Implementation

Process 5 – Establish organisation and develop implementation plans
Activities

5.1 Establish the command control and communications structure

5.2 Develop a framework for business recovery plans

5.3 Develop implementation plans

Process 6 – Implement stand-by arrangements
Activities

6.1 Refine requirements

6.2 Identify and select suppliers

6.3 Integrate solutions

Process 7 – Implement risk reduction measures
Activities

This process is not sub-divided into activities.

Process 8 – Develop business recovery plans
Activities

8.1 Confirm team structures

8.2 Identify tasks and collect reference information

8.3 Produce the plans

Process 9 – Develop procedures
Activities

This process is not sub-divided into activities.

Process 10 – Carry out initial tests
Activities

10.1 Develop test objectives, types and scenarios

10.2 Develop test plans

10.3 Perform tests

10.4 Document and publish test results

Annex A
List of activities by process

Stage 4
Operational management

Process 11 – Testing
Activities

This process is not sub-divided into activities.

Process 12 – Education and awareness
Activities

This process is not sub-divided into activities.

Process 13 – Training
Activities

This process is not sub-divided into activities.

Process 14 – Change Management
Activities

14.1   Determine a change strategy

14.2   Identify the need for change

14.3   Action the changes

14.4   Distribute plans and procedures

Process 15 – Assurance
Activities

This process is not sub-divided into activities.

B Sample product descriptions and quality criteria

This annex provides readers with a number of sample product descriptions. These descriptions relate, in the case of the Project Initiation Document (PID), to products produced to manage projects, and to reports and plans produced by projects that are run to implement business continuity management, as described in this guide. The descriptions detail the purpose of the product, what it should contain, and related quality criteria. The layout of the product descriptions, and some of the terminology used in them, is derived from the PRINCE project management method, but the product descriptions are typical requirements of any project management method.

Samples of the following products are provided:

- Project Initiation Document
- business impact analysis and recovery requirements report
- risk assessment report
- business continuity strategy report
- business recovery plans.

Product no:	Title: Project Initiation Document (PID)

Purpose:

The purpose of this Project Initiation Document is to assist in managing the business continuity management project as effectively as possible. It is one of the main controls to ensure that the cost, schedule and quality targets for BCM are achieved.

Composition:

The PID should include the following:
A statement detailing the terms of reference for the BCM project
A statement describing the scope of the BCM project
The quality review structure that will be implemented to review the deliverables from the BCM project
The project organisational structure that will be used to control the project
A report on the assumptions and risks associated with the project and what mitigating actions can and have been taken
An outline project schedule for each phase of the BCM project
Detailed descriptions for each product from BCM and the quality criteria that will be used to evaluate the products.

Format/presentation:

This should be in accordance with site standards and where appropriate conform to PRINCE standards.

Preceding products:

Terms of reference for the project.

Following products:

Business impact analysis and recovery requirements report, business continuity strategy report, recovery plans, test plans and all other deliverables from the BCM project.

Quality criteria:

1 Are the terms of reference sufficiently comprehensive and clear to enable the BCM project team to understand what is required?
2 Is the scope of the BCM project well documented and is it sufficiently comprehensive to address adequately the BCM requirements for the organisation?
3 Are the proposed project organisation and quality review infrastructures adequate to address the needs of the BCM project?
4 Have all the risks and assumptions associated with the BCM project been adequately identified and described? Have the appropriate actions been taken to address these?
5 Is the project schedule accurate and realistic and is suitable contingency built in?
6 Are all the projects to be delivered described in adequate detail and do the quality criteria allow the reviewers to meet their quality review objectives?

Annex B
Sample product descriptions and quality criteria

Product no:	Title: Business impact analysis and recovery requirements report

Purpose:

The purpose of the business impact analysis and recovery requirements report is to present the results of the business impact analysis to management and to identify both the objectives for maintaining business continuity and the recovery requirements.

Composition:

The business impact analysis and recovery requirements report should include the following:
An overview of the business process or processes that are considered critical to the ongoing survival of the business
A description of the potential business impacts that could occur if the business processes or key components were disrupted
A statement of the proposed recovery objectives for each business process or group of processes to ensure that they operate to a predetermined minimum level of service (identified from the potential business impacts)
A statement of the minimum recovery requirements for each of the critical business processes or components
A brief outline of the recovery options that would enable the objectives and requirements to be met.

Format/presentation:

This should be in accordance with site standards.

Preceding products:

Project Initiation Document.

Following products:

Risk assessment report, business continuity strategy report.

Quality criteria:

1 Have all the critical business processes been adequately identified and described as the basis for understanding the business impacts?
2 Have the potential business impacts been assessed by people who understand the business process and the relationship of the process to the components that support it?
3 Have any seasonal, daily and other variations been taken into account?
4 Are the recovery objectives consistent with the organisation's business objectives?
5 Are the recovery requirements appropriate and sufficiently detailed to enable the recovery options to be identified?
6 Is there a reasonable level of understanding of the various threat scenarios against which recovery objectives and recovery requirements are intended to protect?

Product no:	Title: Risk assessment report

Purpose:

The purpose of the risk assessment report is to enable senior management to understand the extent of risk faced by the organisation. This is done by reviewing the potential business impacts as derived from the business impact analysis and requirements report, against the likelihood of a disaster, or other serious incident occurring, and the organisation's vulnerability to these. The report will identify possible risk reduction measures and help the organisation to determine a balanced risk reduction and recovery strategy.

Composition:

The risk assessment report should include the following:
A description of how the risks were assessed
A description of each risk identified together with an assessment of the likelihood of it occurring and the organisation's vulnerability to it
An assessment of the overall levels of risk to the organisation, taking into account its likelihood of occurrence, the vulnerability and the potential impact
A list of the possible risk reduction measures that would address each of the risks identified.

Format/presentation:

This should be in accordance with site standards.

Preceding products:

Project Initiation Document (PID), business impact analysis and recovery requirements report.

Following products:

Business continuity strategy report, recovery plans, test plans.

Quality criteria:

1 Does the risk assessment comply with the scope of the project as described in the PID?
2 Have a sufficiently comprehensive range of risks been assessed?
3 Are the assessments of likelihood of occurrence and vulnerability realistic and can they be substantiated?
4 Have all the risks been reviewed to identify possible risk reduction measures for further analysis?

Annex B
Sample product descriptions and quality criteria

Product no:	Title: Business continuity strategy report

Purpose:

The purpose of the business continuity strategy report is to document the findings, conclusions and recommendations from the evaluation of the various recovery options and risk reduction measures. This is to provide senior managers with sufficient information to enable them to select appropriate risk reduction and recovery solutions.

Composition:

The business continuity strategy report should include the following:
A description of each recovery option that has been reviewed
An evaluation of each of the recovery options, including an assessment of the advantages and disadvantages of the option together with an indication of cost and a recommendation on which recovery options should be implemented
A description of the risk reduction options that have been considered
A description of the detailed evaluation of each risk reduction option along with appropriate recommendations.

Format/presentation:

This should be in accordance with site standards.

Preceding products:

Project Initiation Document (PID), business impact analysis and recovery requirements report, risk assessment report.

Following products:

Framework of business recovery plans, business recovery plans, test plans.

Quality criteria:

1 Have all the recovery options been adequately identifed and described as the basis for understanding whether they can meet the stated recovery objectives?
2 Have the recovery options been evaluated in sufficient detail to enable a true comparison to be made?
3 Have both the short and long term recovery requirements been addressed by the recommended recovery strategy?
4 Are the recommended recovery strategies and risk reduction measures consistent with the organisation's business objectives?
5 Is there a reasonable level of understanding and agreement as to the various risks that the recommended risk reduction measures are intended to protect against?
6 Have the risk reduction measures been evaluated in sufficient detail to enable a true comparison to be made?

IT Infrastructure Library
A Guide to Business Continuity Management

Product no:	Title: Business recovery plan

Purpose:

The purpose of the business recovery plan(s) is to document the detailed actions that will need to be taken from the moment a disruption occurs. This is to ensure that the stated recovery objectives can be achieved in an orderly and controlled manner.

Composition:

The business recovery plan(s) should include the following:
An overview of the business recovery strategy and objectives that the recovery plans are designed to address
Descriptions of the roles and responsibilities for individuals and teams after a major incident or disruption has occurred
Description of the distinct phases to be followed during recovery
Detailed task list and reference data to be used after a major incident or disruption has occurred
References to other appropriate documentation or plans required during recovery.

Format/presentation:

This should be in accordance with the Framework of business recovery plans or site standards as applicable.

Preceding products:

Project Initiation Document (PID), business continuity strategy report, Framework of business recovery plans.

Following products:

Test plans, change management plans.

Quality criteria:

1 Are the recovery tasks sufficiently comprehensive to enable the recovery objectives to be met?
2 Have all the critical tasks been allocated to individuals or teams?
3 Have the tasks been allocated in such a way as to prevent any one individual having too many tasks to perform?
4 Can the tasks be carried out in sufficient timescales to meet the recovery objectives?
5 Are the plans easy to use and maintain?
6 Is the supporting information accurate and up-to-date?

C Introduction to the business recovery plan template

This template illustrates how a typical business recovery plan could be structured. However, there is no single best solution for structuring plans and the approach taken will reflect the particular requirements of the organisation.

The template has been written in a general fashion so that it will be broadly applicable to all recovery plans that an organisation may wish to produce, ie it can be used for an overall master plan, a computer systems plan, telecommunications plans, plans for individual business processes and even for specialist plans such as salvage, damage assessment etc. The template will, however, need to be tailored for individual plans depending upon their proposed scope and content. A consistent structure (such as that described in the template) should be used for all plans, but the content of each plan may vary. It is recommended that, during the activity, *Define Framework for Business Recovery Plans*, tailored templates are produced for each plan within the set. Detailed plans can then be created by adding information to the templates.

For simplicity, reference information is shown as structured into appendices in this template. Where a plan follows this type of structure, the task lists will refer to appendices where appropriate. Some organisations may find it more useful to integrate reference information within the task lists.

Some business continuity planning software tools dictate the plan format whilst others allow the user to define the optimum plan layout.

The template shows chapter headings and some typical table layouts. Brief descriptions of each section are included in italics.

References in square brackets refer to guidance or examples in the text of this guide.

IT Infrastructure Library
A Guide to Business Continuity Management

ABC Organisation

Business recovery plan template for the XYZ processes

Copy no:

PLAN OWNER

This plan is owned by ***** who is responsible for ensuring that it remains up to date.

CHANGE RECORD

Issue number	Date	Issued by	Reason for Issue

DISTRIBUTION LIST

Copy	Issued to	Copy	Issued to
1		13	
2		14	
3		15	
4		16	
5		17	
6		18	
7		19	
8		20	
9		21	
10		22	
11		23	
12		24	

Annex C
ABC Organisation – business recovery plan template for the XYZ Processes

Table of Contents

1. ABC Organisation's integrated business recovery plans
    1.1 Background
    1.2 Purpose of the plans
    1.3 The phases of recovery
    1.4 Structure of the plans

2. Organisation for the business recovery plan
    2.1 Introduction
    2.2 Roles and responsibilities
    2.3 Communications

3. Task lists for the master plan
    3.1 Alert phase
        3.1.1 Actions to initiate the recovery
            3.1.1.1 Out of normal hours
            3.1.1.2 During normal hours
        3.1.2 Actions on receipt of the initial report from the scene
        3.1.3 Actions if the Alert phase is continued
        3.1.4 Alert phase task lists
            3.1.4.1 $$ $$ CO-ORDINATOR
        3.1.5 Alert phase tasks
    3.2 Invocation and recovery phase
        3.2.1 Invocation and recovery phase task lists
            3.2.1.1 $$ $$ CO-ORDINATOR
    3.3 Return to normal phase

APPENDIX A – TEAM MEMBERS

APPENDIX B – KEY CONTACT DETAILS

    B1 Recovery team members and deputies

    B2 Board members

    B3 Staff

APPENDIX C – EMERGENCY CONTROL CENTRES

    C1 Location of the ECCs

    C2 Minimum facilities and equipment for the ECCs

APPENDIX D – RECOVERY OBJECTIVES AND MINIMUM REQUIREMENTS

APPENDIX E – RECOVERY STRATEGY AND STAND-BY ARRANGEMENTS

APPENDIX F – OTHER CONTACTS

APPENDIX G – PROCEDURES

APPENDIX H – STAND-BY SITES

    H1 Map of the location(s)

    H2 Allocation of accommodation

    H3 Schedule of assets required

APPENDIX I – ASSET REGISTER

APPENDIX J – DRAFT STATEMENTS FOR ISSUE TO INTERESTED PARTIES

APPENDIX K – FORMS

APPENDIX L – CHECKLISTS

    L1 Damage assessment checklist

    L2 Other checklists

APPENDIX M – DOCUMENTATION

Annex C
ABC Organisation – business recovery plan template for the XYZ Processes

1 ABC Organisation's integrated business recovery plans

1.1 Background

Describing the need for the plan and the risks that it addresses. Possibly including a business continuity strategy statement and a summary of the key elements of the strategy.

1.2 Purpose of the plans

Describing the purpose of the plans, eg to prepare the organisation to cope with emergencies, and to define:

- *the roles and responsibilities of the individuals and teams that will be involved in the recovery*
- *lists of tasks to be carried out*
- *the necessary reference information to support the actions detailed in the task lists.*

The plans will guide the organisation through the many activities that are necessary to achieve its recovery objectives.

1.3 The phases of recovery

Describing the phases of recovery, eg

- **ALERT** *phase during which:*
  - *an incident is reported*
  - *an initial damage assessment is completed*
  - *a decision is taken to move to the invocation and recovery phase*

- **INVOCATION AND RECOVERY** *phase during which:*
  - *stand-by arrangements are implemented*
  - *stand-by arrangements are operated*
  - *business processes are recovered*

- **RETURN TO NORMAL** *phase during which:*
  - *the 'return to normal' is planned*
  - *accommodation, systems, telecommunications and other equipment are refurbished, repaired or replaced*
  - *operations transfer from the stand-by arrangements to the permanent arrangements*
  - *the recovery is declared to be complete and the business recovery teams stand down.*

The plan will place most emphasis on the first two phases which are likely to be carried out within strict time constraints.
[See 5.1, sub-section, Develop a framework for business recovery plans]

1.4 Structure of the plans

Describing the integrated set of business recovery plans and where this particular plan fits within the set. Possibly including a diagram.
[See 5.1, sub-section, Develop a framework for business recovery plans]

IT Infrastructure Library
A Guide to Business Continuity Management

2 Organisation for the business recovery plan

2.1 Introduction

Providing an overview of how recovery will be co-ordinated following a major incident. Describing the central co-ordination team and the business recovery teams. Referring to the Emergency Control Centre (ECC).
[See 5.1, sub-section, Establish command, control and communications structure]

2.2 Roles and responsibilities

Describing the roles and responsibilities of the team members that will use this particular plan.
[See 5.1, sub-section, Establish command, control and communications structure]

2.3 Communications

Describing how communications will be maintained during the recovery effort and where authority will rest.
[See 5.1, sub-section, Establish command, control and communications structure]

Annex C
ABC Organisation – business recovery plan template for the XYZ Processes

3 Task lists for the master plan

3.1 Alert phase

3.1.1 Actions to initiate the recovery

3.1.1.1 Out of normal hours

Describing the lines of communication, responsibilities and immediate actions to be taken if an incident occurs outside normal working hours.

3.1.1.2 During normal hours

Describing the lines of communication, responsibilities and immediate actions to be taken if an incident occurs during normal working hours.

3.1.2 Actions on receipt of the initial report from the scene

Describing the actions to be taken on receipt of the initial report from the scene. This will either be to invoke the stand-by arrangements and commence recovery or to continue with the Alert phase until further information becomes available.

3.1.3 Actions if the Alert phase is continued

Describing the actions to be undertaken if the Alert phase is continued, typically damage assessment, salvage, communications etc. To include a description of the conditions under which invocation will be ordered.

3.1.4 Alert phase task lists

Including a prioritised list of tasks for the business recovery team, possibly including a separate list for each member of the business recovery team. A typical structure for each task list is shown on the following page. Tasks for the Alert phase are shown starting at number 05 and increasing in increments of 5 (to allow additional tasks to be added without the need for renumbering all tasks). Tasks for each member of the team will be prefixed with a code for the team member, eg IT05 would be the first task for the IT co-ordinator in the Alert phase. The general prefix $$ is used in the example overleaf.

3.1.5 Alert phase tasks

Figure 14 contains a list of typical Alert phase tasks.

IT Infrastructure Library
A Guide to Business Continuity Management

3.1.4.1 $$ $$ CO-ORDINATOR	Task allocated to	Time completed
$$05		
$$10		
$$15		
$$20		
$$25		
$$30		
$$35		
$$40		

3.2 Invocation and recovery phase

Describing the immediate actions to be taken once a decision has been taken to invoke the stand-by arrangements.

3.2.1 Invocation and recovery phase task lists

Including a prioritised list of tasks for the business recovery team, possibly including a separate list for each member of the business recovery team. A typical structure for each task list is shown on the following page. Tasks for the INVOCATION AND RECOVERY phase are shown starting at number 105 and increasing in increments of 5 (to allow additional tasks to be added without the need for renumbering all tasks). Tasks for each member of the team will be prefixed with a code for the team member, eg IT105 would be the first task for the IT co-ordinator in the recovery and invocation phase. The general prefix $$ is used in the example overleaf.

3.2.2 Invocation and recovery phase tasks

Figure 14 contains a list of typical invocation and recovery phase tasks.

IT Infrastructure Library
A Guide to Business Continuity Management

3.2.1.1 $$ $$ CO-ORDINATOR	Task allocated to	Time completed
RM105		
RM110		
RM115		
RM120		
RM125		
RM130		
RM135		
RM140		

3.3 Return to normal phase

Describing the actions involved in planning and implementing the return to normal operations, eg:

- *confirming the timescales for refurbishment of damaged accommodation or identifying alternative permanent accommodation*
- *organising the furnishing and equipping of the site*
- *organising the installation of telecommunications equipment and services*
- *organising the installation of systems and networks*
- *organising the phased transfer of staff from the stand-by sites to the permanent accommodation*
- *communicating with staff, customers, suppliers, the media etc.*

APPENDIX A – TEAM MEMBERS

Identifying team members and their deputies.

Role:	Name:	First deputy:	Second deputy:

APPENDIX B – KEY CONTACT DETAILS

B1 Recovery team members and deputies

Contact details for team members and deputies, eg home address, telephone, fax, mobile, pager numbers.

B2 Board members

Contact details for Board members.

B3 Staff

Contact details for other key staff, possibly including a 'cascade' system of communications where each manager or nominated member of staff is responsible for contacting subordinate staff.

APPENDIX C – EMERGENCY CONTROL CENTRES

C1 Location of the ECCs

Including a map and access arrangements for the ECCs.

C2 Minimum facilities and equipment for an ECC

Describing the minimum facilities and equipment required at the ECC.

Annex C
ABC Organisation – business recovery plan template for the XYZ Processes

APPENDIX D – RECOVERY OBJECTIVES AND MINIMUM REQUIREMENTS

Describing the recovery objectives and minimum requirements for the processes covered by the plan.
[See 4.1, sub-sections, Define business recovery objectives and Assess minimum requirements]

IT Infrastructure Library
A Guide to Business Continuity Management

APPENDIX E – RECOVERY STRATEGY AND STAND-BY ARRANGEMENTS

Describing the recovery strategy and the stand-by arrangements that have been put in place to support this.

[See 4.3, sub-section, Define overall strategy]

Annex C
ABC Organisation – business recovery plan template for the XYZ Processes

APPENDIX F - OTHER CONTACTS

Including other essential contact details, eg emergency services, loss adjusters, key customers, suppliers, disaster recovery services, salvage companies, media contacts, major shareholders.

Organisation:	Contact name:	Telephone no, fax no, email address etc:	Address:

APPENDIX G - PROCEDURES

Including (or referring to) any procedures necessary to support the task lists.

APPENDIX H – STAND-BY SITES

H1 Map of the location(s)

Including a map and access arrangements for stand-by sites.

H2 Allocation of accommodation

Including or referring to floor plans and stand-by sites showing the proposed locations for individual business functions. Possibly also showing power and telephone sockets, computer network access points etc.

H3 Schedule of assets required

Description of the assets required at stand-by sites. These will either be provided in advance or obtained as quickly as possible once invocation is ordered.

APPENDIX I - ASSET REGISTER

Including or referring to a register of critical assets held at the original sites. To assist with the identification of assets for damage assessment and salvage as well as for insurance purposes. May be available in a configuration management database - see the IT Infrastructure Library module **Configuration Management**.

Annex C
ABC Organisation – business recovery plan template for the XYZ Processes

APPENDIX J – DRAFT STATEMENTS FOR ISSUE TO INTERESTED PARTIES

Including draft statements to the media, customers, suppliers etc that can be tailored and distributed quickly following an incident.

APPENDIX K – FORMS

Including or referring to forms that will be required to support the recovery effort.

APPENDIX L – CHECKLISTS

L1 Damage assessment checklist

A checklist of items to check during the damage assessment.

L2 Other checklists

Other checklists that will be required to support the recovery effort.

APPENDIX M – DOCUMENTATION

Describing the location of any documents referred to, but not included within, the business recovery plan.

Document title:	Location:	Contact:	Notes:

D Example application of Annual Loss Expectancy (ALE)

> **Important Note**
> The following example is provided for illustrative purposes. It elaborates on the information contained in section 4.3 on the financial evaluation of recovery options. Owing to the difficulty and danger in using quantitative assessments of risk, great care should be taken when using this type of calculation. Expert advice should be sought before recommendations derived from an ALE analysis are acted on.

Consider an organisation without any business recovery measures in place and assume that the potential impact from a terrorist blast, major fire or other disaster is estimated at £100 million.

Assume also that the likelihood of such an incident occurring is estimated at once in every 50 years.

$$\text{ALE} = £100\text{m}/50 = £2 \text{ million per year}$$

If recovery measures costing £1 million per year were introduced and reduced the potential impact to £20 million the ALE would be reduced to £0.4 million.

The annual *nett saving* from introduction of the recovery measures is therefore:

	Original ALE	£2m per year
–	New ALE	£0.4m per year
–	Cost of Measures	£1m per year
=	Nett savings per annum	£0.6m per year

Under the ALE evaluation, the recovery measures proposed would be considered to be justified.

In practice, it is unlikely that organisations will have more than a few options that can satisfy the broad recovery objectives and be taken forward for a comparative evaluation. Often, the choice of option comes down to a question of whether to select an expensive option to guarantee that recovery objectives could be met, or to select a less expensive option where there is a risk that objectives will not be met. In considering this choice it is useful to consider how the potential *saving* varies with risk.

With reference to the above example, the annual saving from introduction of recovery measures can be stated as:

Annual saving	=	ALE without measure	–	ALE with measure	–	Cost of measure

This can be represented graphically as illustrated in the attached figure which shows how the annual saving varies with risk (measured in this case as the estimated time between incidents). Option 1 becomes cost effective when the risk exceeds 1 in 34 years, whereas the risk would need to be greater than 1 in 12 years for Option 2 to be justified.

175

IT Infrastructure Library
A Guide to Business Continuity Management

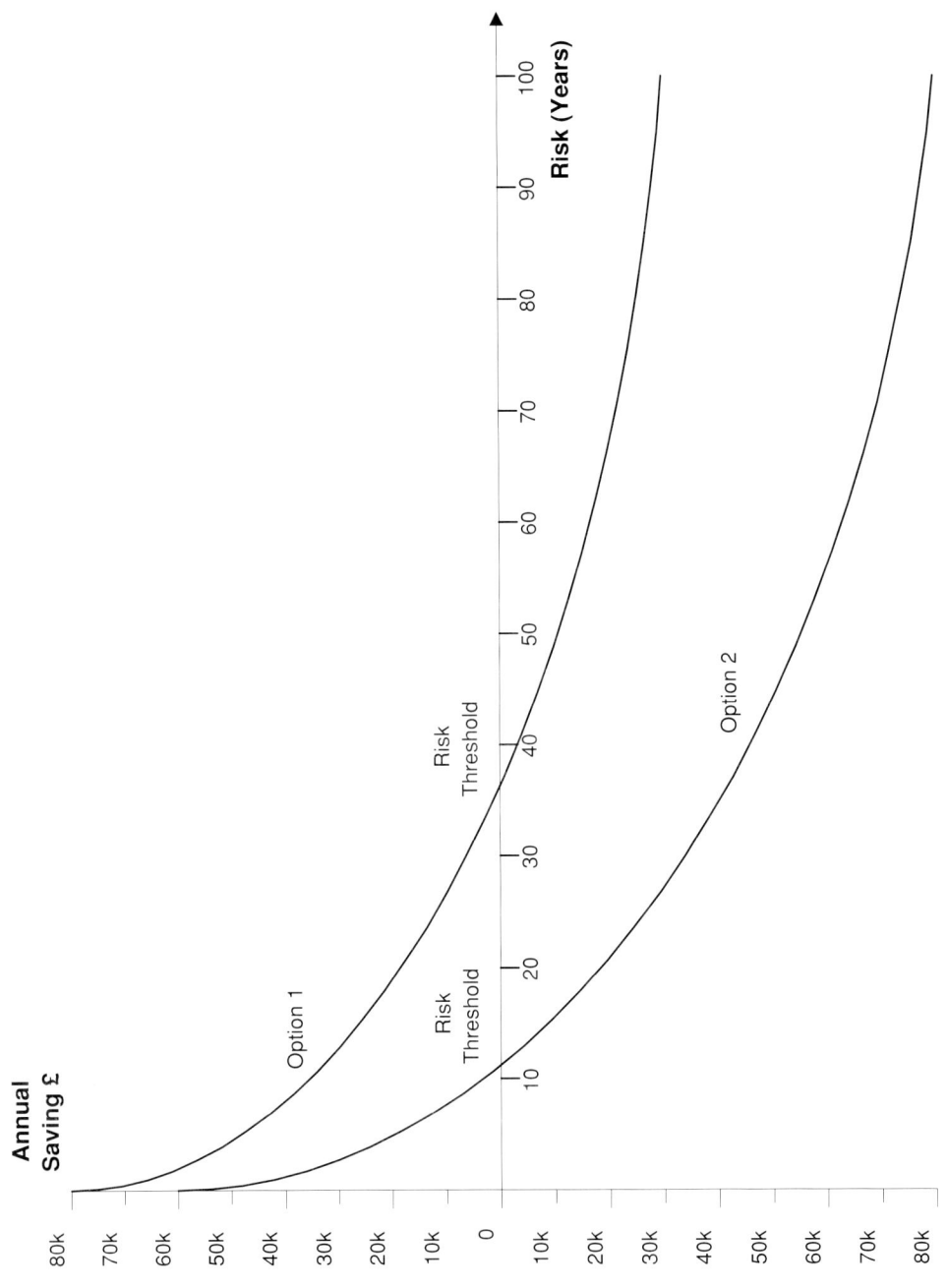

Figure 17 Variation on benefit with risk

Index

Alert phase 55, 153, 155, 157
assurance 83, 93, 94, 95, 107, 128, 141
audit 17, 60, 94, 95, 100, 107, 127, 128
authority 53, 54, 126
awareness 9

back-up 60, 70, 77, 78
BS7799 15
business continuity management
    definition of 7
    lifecycle 11, 12, 16
    process model 13, 14
Business Continuity Manager 51, 83, 87, 88, 90, 92, 94, 100
business functions 8, 11, 22, 46, 109, 122, 123, 125, 126
centralised 7, 109, 110, 111, 113, 115, 118
business impact analysis 16, 21, 22, 23, 24, 28, 38
business process re-engineering 23
business processes 7, 8, 11, 12, 16, 17, 21, 22
business recovery plan 12, 49, 55, 58, 59, 63, 76 105, 140
business recovery teams 50, 53, 68, 88, 99, 114, 156

central co-ordination team 50, 51, 53, 54, 57, 64, 67, 68, 83, 87, 93, 99, 114, 156
change control 17, 46, 86, 94, 100, 107, 120, 121, 127
change management 83, 86, 87, 88
co-ordination 15, 57, 67, 122
command, control and communications 16, 49, 50, 57, 59, 62, 119, 156
commitment 9, 15, 18, 84, 86, 95
configuration management 46
contingency planning 7, 15, 30, 102, 105
core team 61, 64, 103, 113, 121
CRAMM 18, 27, 30, 38, 48, 63, 103, 104
crisis management 51, 55, 57, 59, 66, 71, 119, 127

damage assessment 55, 57, 66, 68, 69, 119, 149, 155, 157, 170, 173
decision making 86, 97, 99, 101
decontamination 69
distributed business process 117

education 16, 17, 53, 66, 83, 85, 86, 93, 101, 107
emergency control centre 60, 127
emergency response 46, 55, 59, 66, 67
evacuation 67

hard impact 25, 26
Health and Safety Executive 69

impact scenario 24, 25, 27, 34, 139
implementation plan 49, 59, 64, 104, 140
implementation stage 49, 59, 79, 86, 99, 104
incident reporting 46
information model 23
initiation 9, 15, 66, 102
insurance 12, 27, 39, 46, 48, 69, 112, 170
invocation 55, 62, 67, 80, 115, 155, 159, 169
Invocation and recovery phase 67, 155, 159

legal responsibility 70
loss adjuster 46, 69, 167

management/executive Board 51, 54, 67, 71, 99
master plan 57, 59, 64, 66, 67, 87, 157
media 71
methods 7, 9, 85, 101, 102, 103, 104, 106
milestones 95

operational management stage 83, 100
organisation and control 15, 18, 105, 139
outsourced business function 122
outsourced business process 122
ownership 87, 106

phases 55, 63, 153, 155
policy 12, 15, 16, 17, 83, 84, 102, 128, 139
PRINCE 18, 59, 63, 97, 102, 105, 143
profit 27
Project Initiation Document 19, 143
project manager 18
project plan 8, 19
public relations 51, 53, 57, 59, 66, 71, 86, 119, 127

quality plan 15, 19, 94, 139
quality review 18, 19

Index

Recovery Manager 51, 54, 67, 87, 88
recovery options 39, 109, 110, 111, 118, 126
    loss of critical paper records 39, 69, 70, 118
    loss of data 39, 69, 70, 121
    loss of PABX or ACD services 55
    loss of PABX or ACD systems 39, 64, 118
    loss of power 39, 112
    loss of computer systems or networks 64, 113
    unavailability of key staff 39, 114, 118
recovery planning 105, 106, 107
recovery services 16, 39, 60, 61, 104, 167
reference information 64
regulators 51
requirements and strategy stage 62, 97, 99, 100, 102, 116
resilience 37, 46, 112, 117, 120, 122, 125
resources 17
responsibility 8
Return to normal phase 67
risk assessment 16, 21, 30, 38, 48, 95, 103, 109, 123, 124, 125, 139
    qualitative 38
    quantitative 37, 38, 175
risk reduction 46, 47, 49, 62, 104, 109, 111, 114, 117, 120, 125, 127
risk reduction options
    bomb protection 111
    control over physical access 111
    critical electronic media 118
    fire protection 111
    flood protection 111
    loss of power 112
    protection of incoming services 111
    protection of vital electronic or manual media 111
    virus protection 117
    vital paper records 118
risks
    damage or denial of access 11, 110, 117
    failure of service providers 103
    loss of computer systems 104, 110, 116, 123, 124
    loss of critical paper records 104
    loss of data 70
    loss of power 34, 111
    unavailability of key staff 11, 114
roles 51, 63, 64

salvage 69

scope 16, 63, 102, 109, 110, 115, 116, 122
security cordon 69
service level agreements 123, 125
single point of failure 110, 111, 122
skills 7, 9, 18, 97, 98, 99, 100, 102
soft impact 25, 26, 27
software 60, 78, 101, 105, 106, 149
SSADM 105
steering committee 18, 123

task list 63, 66, 72, 77, 94, 149, 153, 157, 168
techniques 7, 9, 18, 97, 98, 99, 100, 102
template 59, 63, 100, 105, 106, 149, 151
terms of reference 15, 16, 17, 19, 102, 109, 110, 115, 139
testing
    full tests 84, 115
    objectives 84, 85, 94, 127, 140
    of business components 84, 115
    of technical components 115
    plans 17, 106
    programmes 86
    scenarios 127, 140
    walkthrough 84, 93
threats 34, 37, 38, 48, 93, 103
tools 7, 9, 101, 102, 103, 104, 105, 106, 107, 149
training 86,

vital records 57, 66, 68, 70, 113, 117, 121, 127
vulnerability (ies) 34, 103
vulnerability factors 103

working groups 19, 98